DESIGNS OF WINDOWS

PUSTAK MAHAL®

Administrative office and sale centre
J-3/16 , Daryaganj, New Delhi-110002
☎ 23276539, 23272783, 23272784 • *Fax:* 011-23260518
E-mail: info@pustakmahal.com • *Website:* www.pustakmahal.com

Branches
Bengaluru: ☎ 080-22234025 • *Telefax:* 080-22240209
E-mail: pustak@airtelmail.in • pustak@sancharnet.in
Mumbai: ☎ 022-22010941, 022-22053387
E-mail: rapidex@bom5.vsnl.net.in
Patna: ☎ 0612-3294193 • *Telefax:* 0612-2302719
E-mail: rapidexptn@rediffmail.com

ISBN 978-81-223-0526-5

Edition: 2014

Printed at : **Radha Offset Delhi**

DESIGNS OF WINDOWS

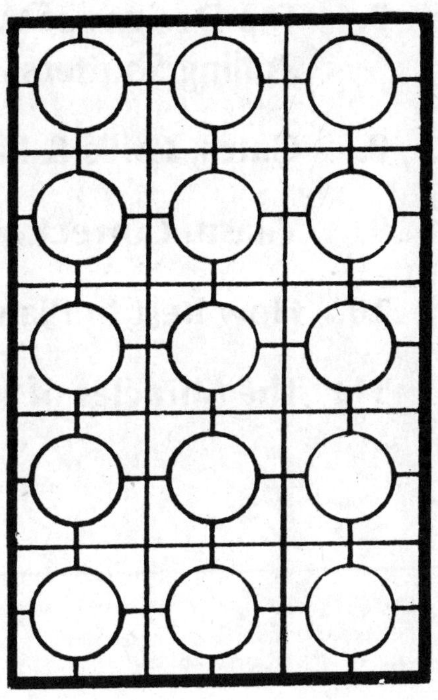

Other books in this series

1.	New Steel Furniture Catalogue	195.00
2.	More and More Designs of Gates, Grills, Railings & Staircases	100.00
3.	Designs of Railings	100.00
4.	Designs of Railings	100.00
5.	Designs of Windows	100.00
6.	Designs of Gates	100.00
7.	Top Designs of Windos Grills & Rolling Shutters	100.00
8.	Gates, Grills & Railing Sets	100.00
9.	Vaastu Corrections without Demolitions	100.00
10.	How Best to Plan & Build Your Home	175.00
11.	The Miracles of Vaastu Shastra	195.00

Pustak Mahal

Beautiful Window

Art of Mughal Period
Designs

simple and ornamental design. In the Centre, simple and ornamental design has been used.

Latest

Japan's design for beauty &

Exhibition purpose.

Ornamental designs using thinner flats for the decoration.

A carpet type Design using squares and billas in order and reverse in the alternate space.

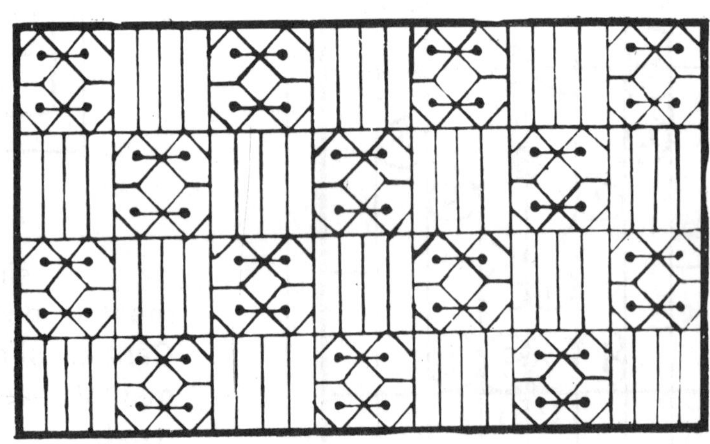

Two universal window

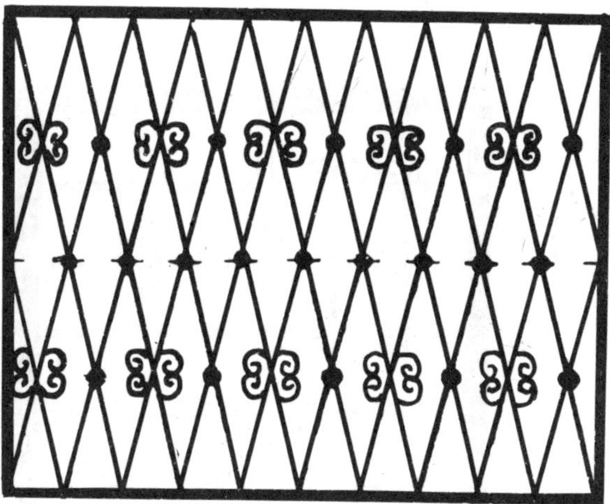

This is the most suitable design Ornamental for all types of buildings.

New and best Emposition of modern design of net and solid rod adjustment.

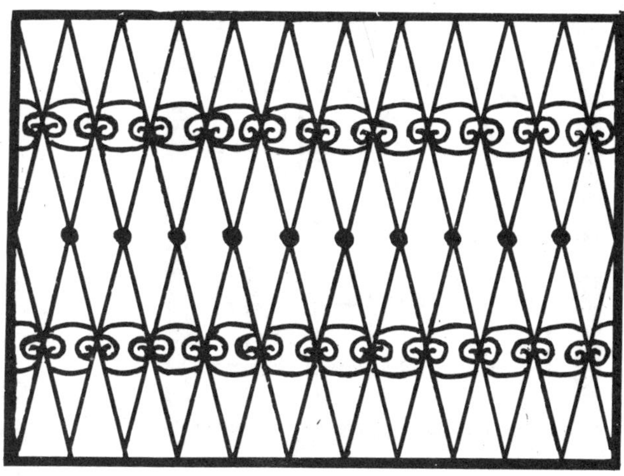

Beautiful Window

This is a beautiful window Grill Design using circles and billas for the decoration. A Common height of the window is 4'. The gap may be given according to the choice.

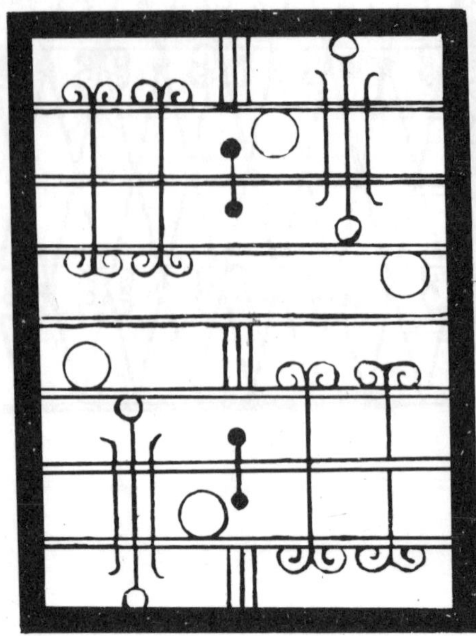

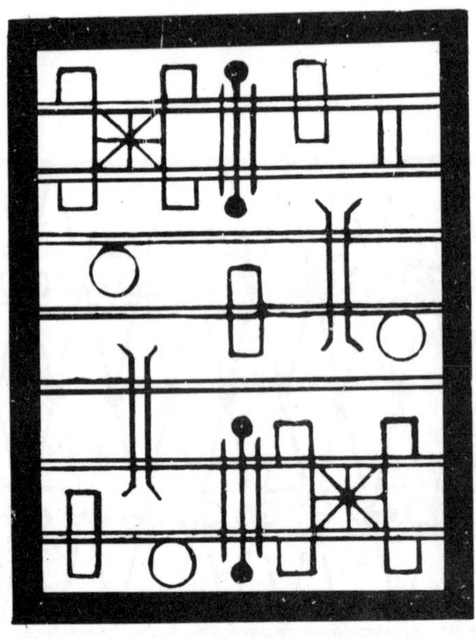

Best and universal design of steel sheet cutting and solid iron bars.

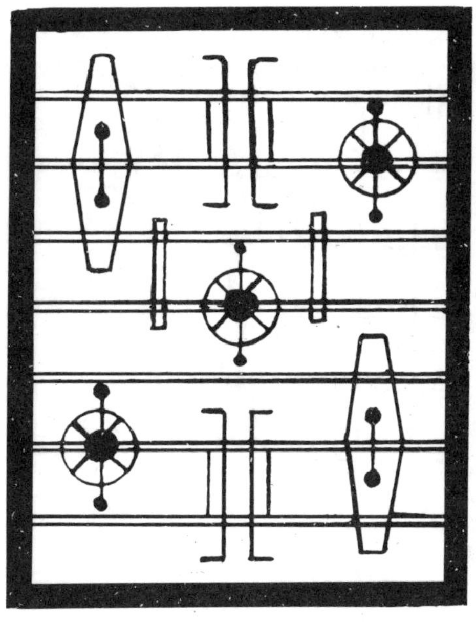

Symitrical setting of Semicircle and straight Iron bars design, for window Grill

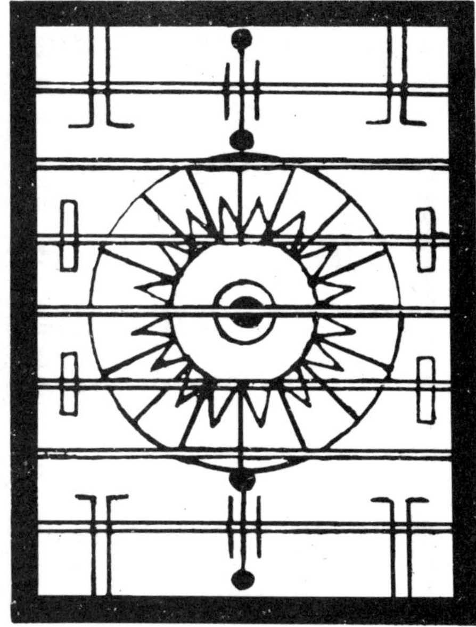

Latest and universal Sunflower design of famous Indian style for Strong Construction.

New design of Paris

Latest and universal Sunflower design of famous Indian style for Strong Construction.

Latest German designs of M. S. wrought Iron bars with still or Net pieces insertion.

Latest Designs of straight Square Bars.

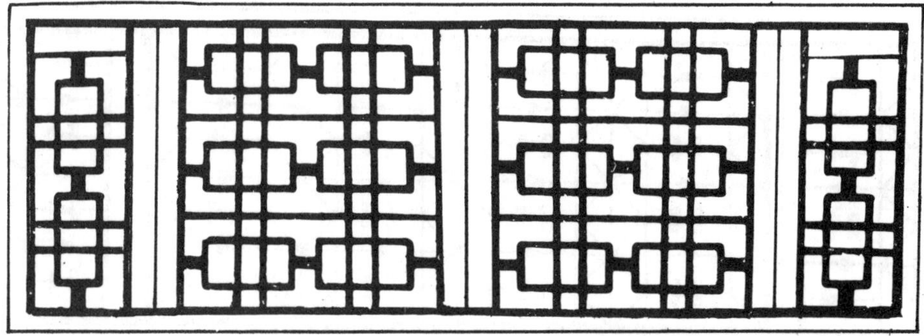

Thick and thin vertical Iron bar Designs for big factories workshop and House

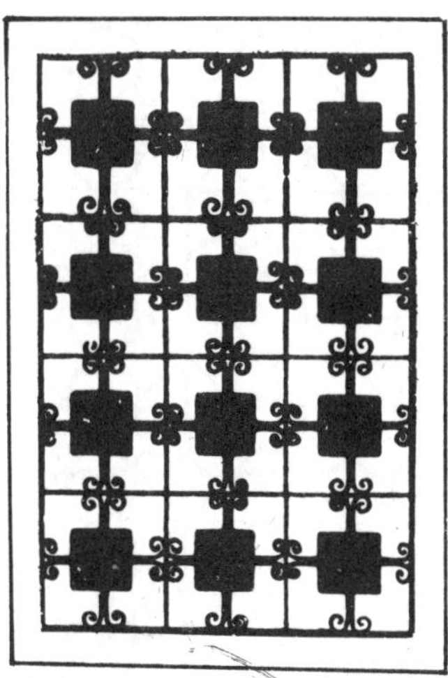

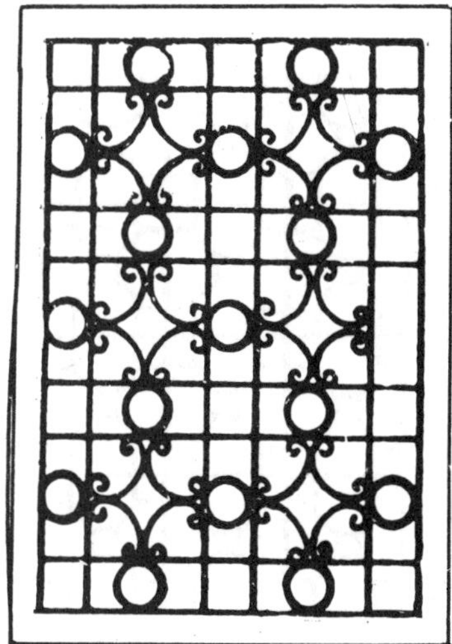

Switzerland design for window Grill.

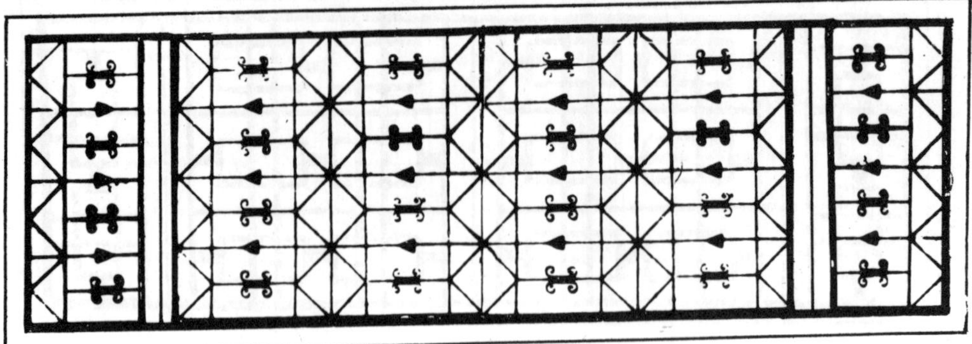

British Ancient Art suitable for office, College and School Buildings.

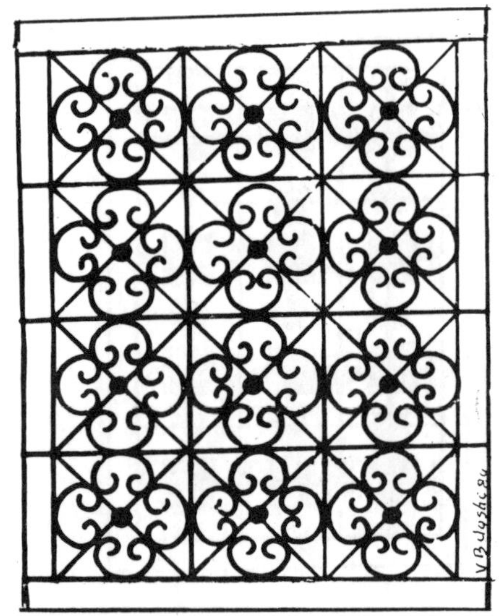

window Grill.

Universal designs for Good Building

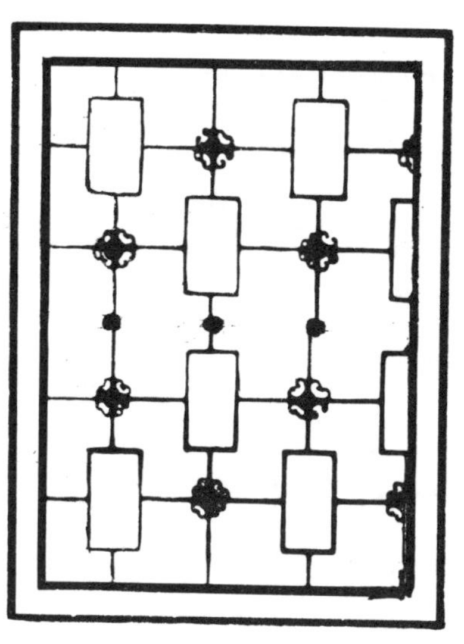

Design in Modern style is the way of modern life.

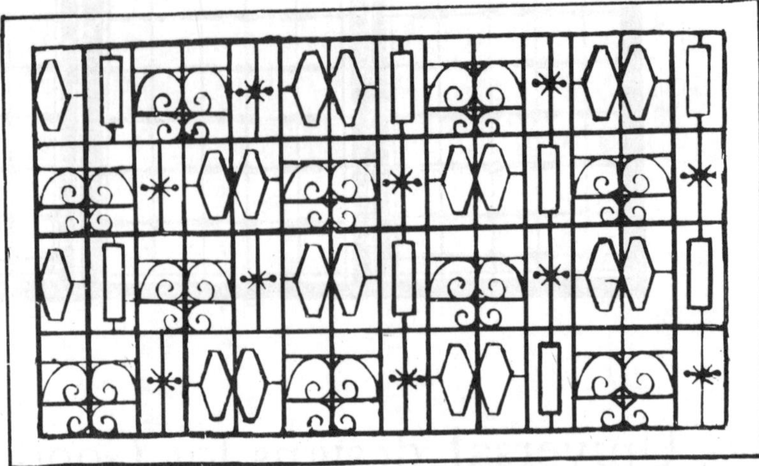

Kite type design with beautiful decoration

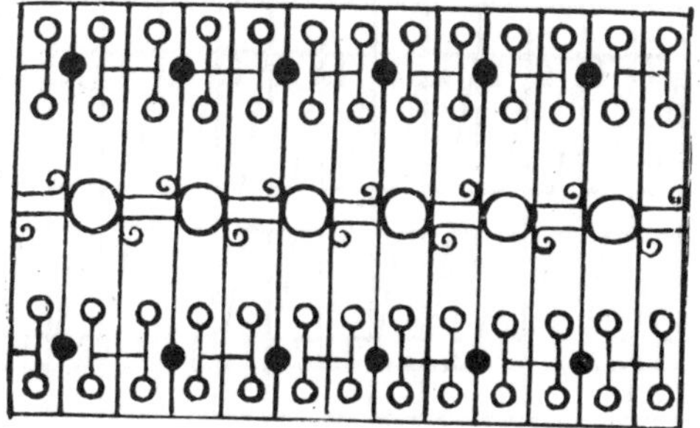

Old Style with Modern Touch design using thinner flats for the decoration.

A New simple and straight cutting lines design using squares and billas.

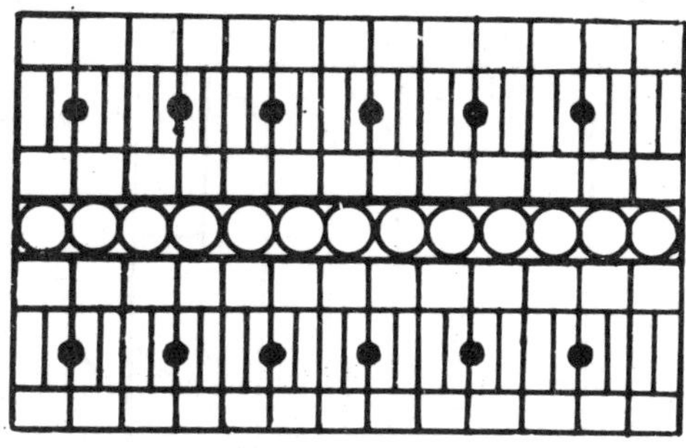

A new Attraction of Italian · This is a Simple type Design using "O" types and squares. It looks simple and beautiful.

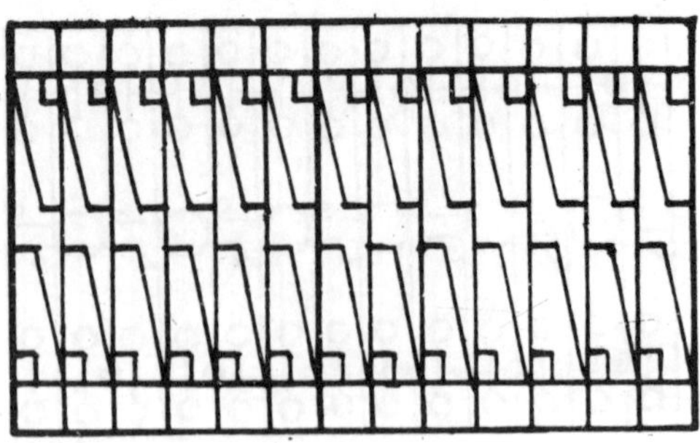

New and simple box type design fully support of closer type in the bottom space.

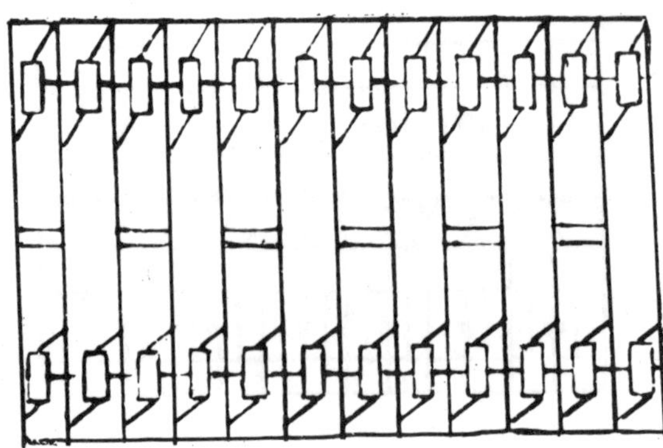

Common for all types Designs of U. K. for window railing etc. Leaving Gap of 4" between Two square Rods

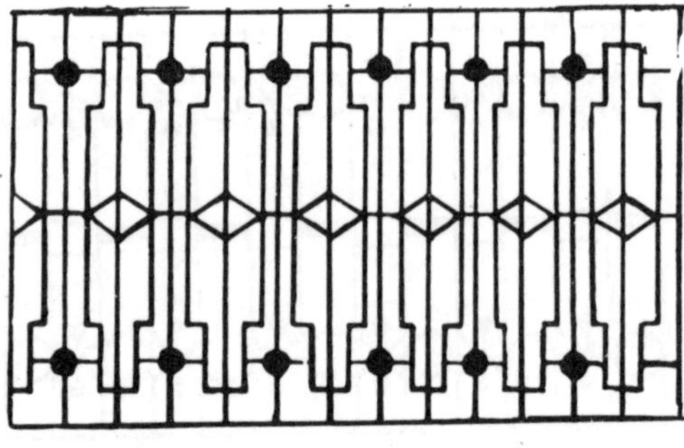

Simple royal design using thinner flats and billas. The gap of 4" in between two square rods or flats may be given.

Straight Iron bar designs of Germany

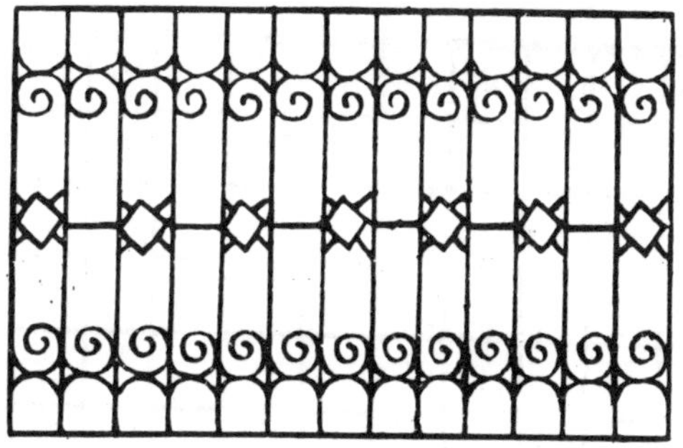

Latest ornamental type design using thinner flats for the decoration suits for all types of buildings

Latest, simple and beautiful design. of iron bars This is the most suitable for all types of buildings.

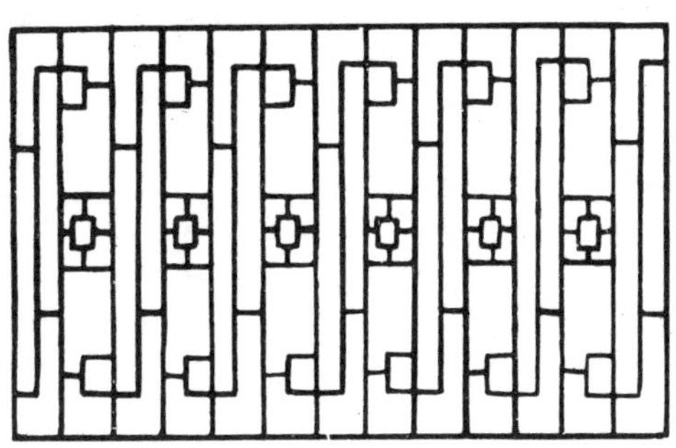

Straight Design of Germany. suitable for varandah Grill The square rods or flats may be used for vertical position.

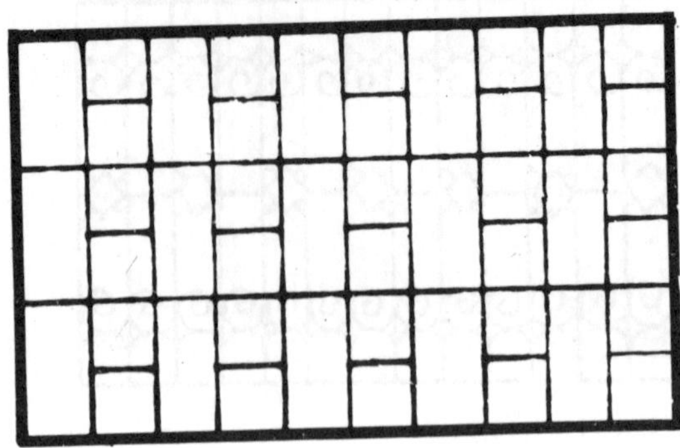

Very Cheerful design for House and Garden Fancing.

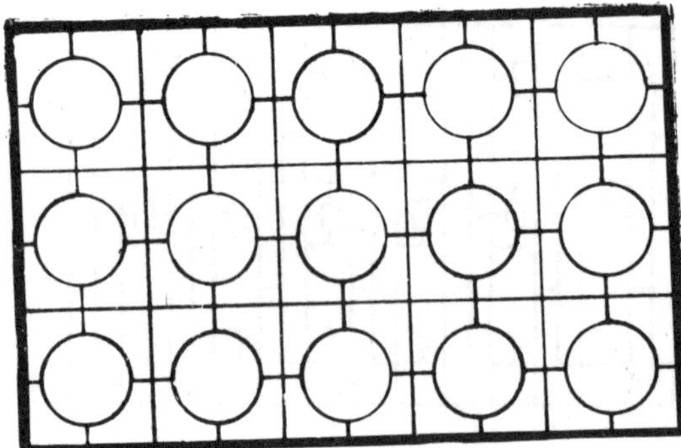

Latest design of solid Iron bars in square and circular style for window,

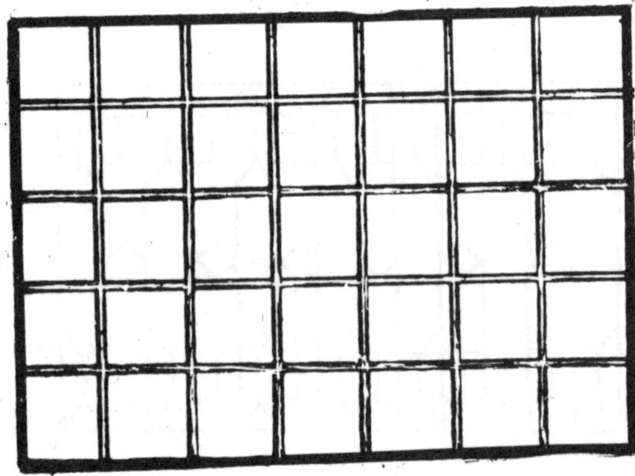

Square and flate Steel Bars design of windows for Front side of Building

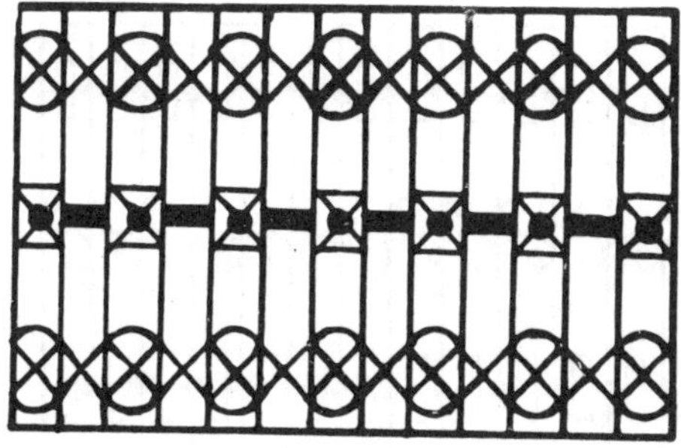

Japan's Design for varandah grill using squares in small and big sizes. This type is also useful for the plaster of paris, carpet and textiles decoration.

Very Cheerful design for House and Garden Fancing.

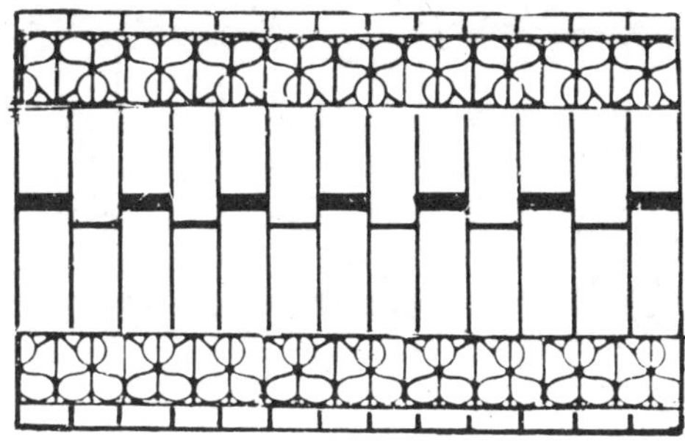

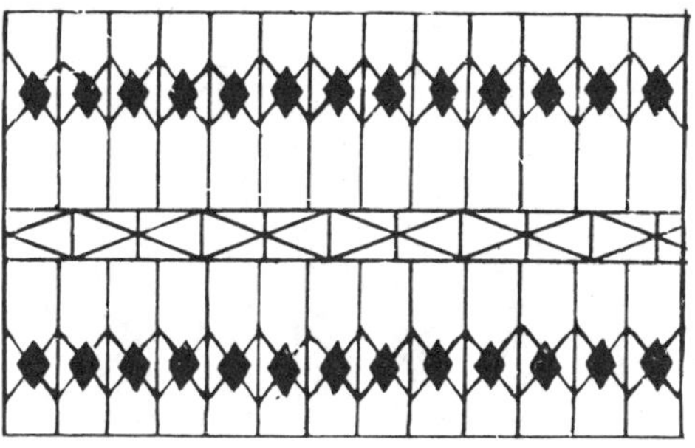

Best universal Ornamental design using triangles and squares with fully support for more strength

A Beauti ful Design of Modern art. In this design Flowers 'S' types and rectangular types are used.

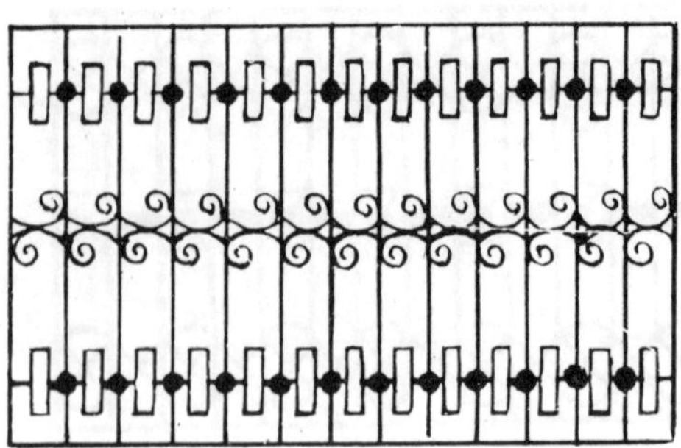

Most attractive fine art latest type design using diamonds, rectangular and other ornamentals.

A beautiful " Peacock " type design. most suitable for domestic and Industrial buildings.

New Circular Designs of Iron bars

Steel Bar Frames with Artistic Cutting adjustment.

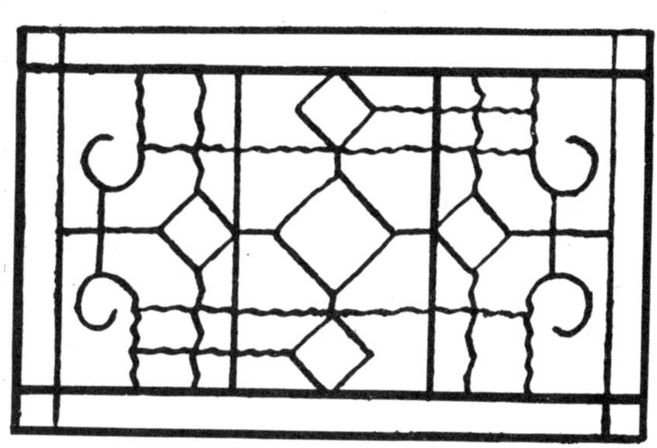

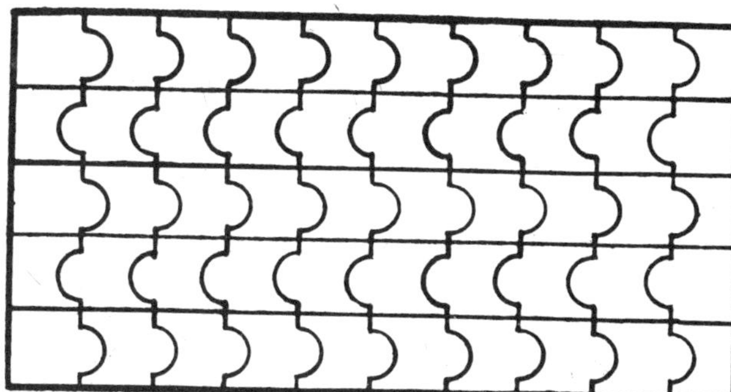

Symitrical setting of Semicircle and straight Iron bars design.

West Germany's Designs of Windows and Ventilators

This is a simple and beautiful Design, Circles, Semi circles and billas are used. for the safety and decoration.

A beautiful window Grill Design using circles and billas for the decoration.

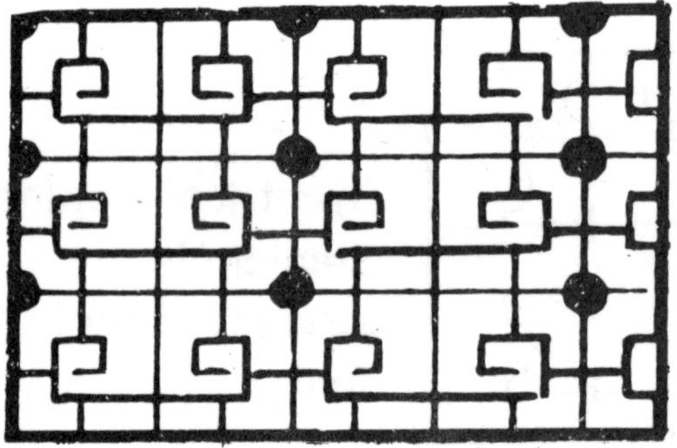

Latest and universal **Rectangular** design of famous Indian style for Strong Construction.

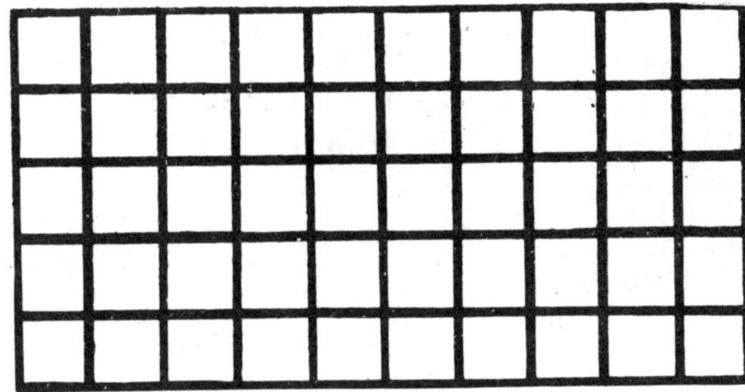

Cheapest Solid rods design for the simple decoration purposes. The gap of 4" between two square rods or flats may be given.

Modern simple and beautiful design.

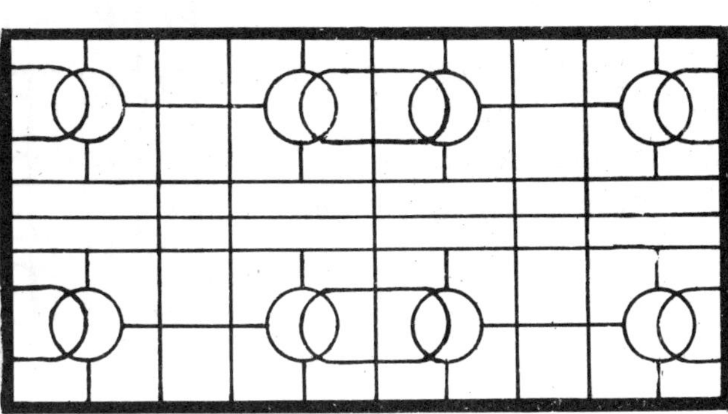

Symitrical design of straight solid iron bars for Strong Construction.

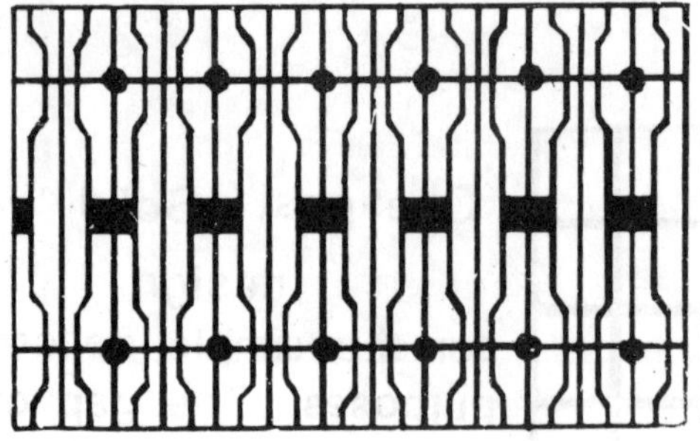

A new Attraction of Italian latest type of design and suits for all the latest types of buildings.

Beautiful Japanese Design. In this window Grill Design, the squares, and diamonds types are given

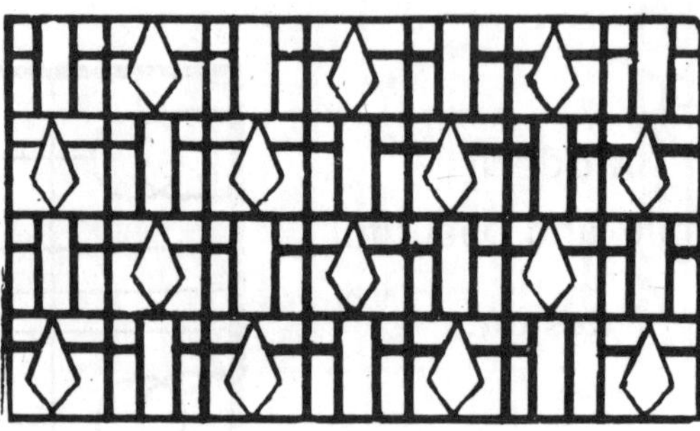

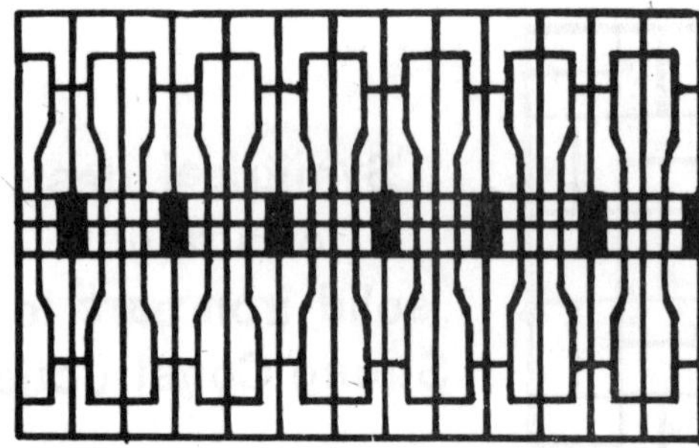

A Common design for commercial House Residential Building, Shop and Factories etc.

West-Germany's Design for Biggest Construction. using thinner flats and billas for the decoration purposes.

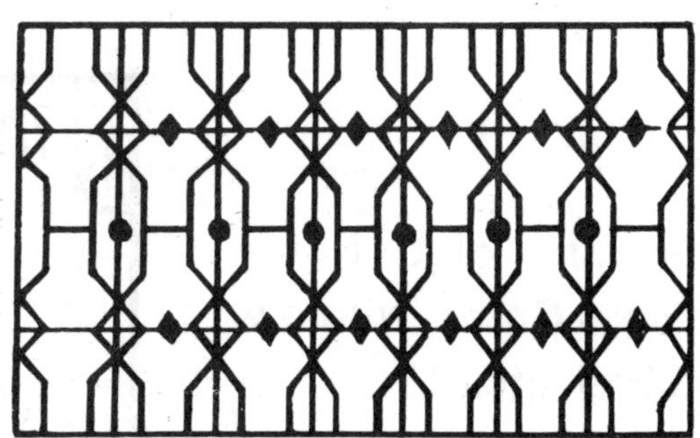

Straight Iron Bars **design suits both** for the domestic **and Industrial** buildings.

Very Beautiful Design of Modern Decoration **This type of design suits both** for the domestic **and Industrial** buildings.

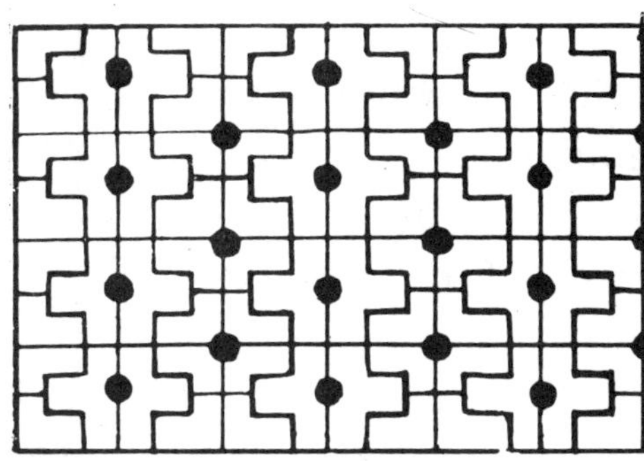

Beautiful Window

Designs of U. K. for Iron Gate. window railing etc.

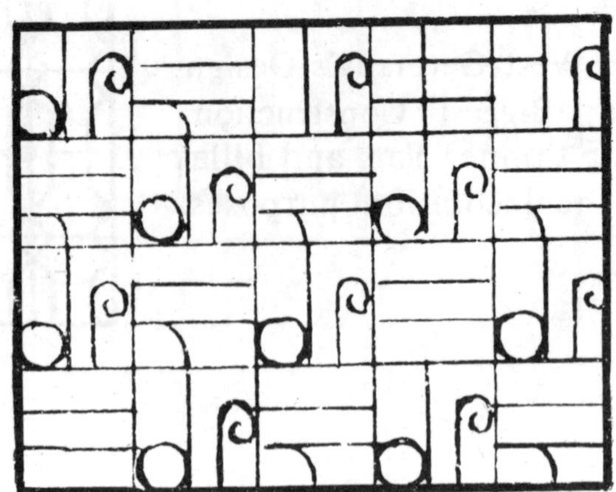

Latest German designs of M. S. wrought Iron bars

Symitrical setting of Semicircle and straight Iron bars design for window Grill

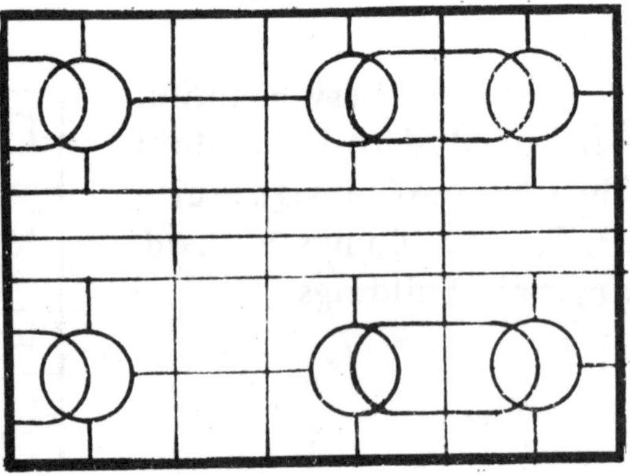

Latest Designs of straight Square Bars.

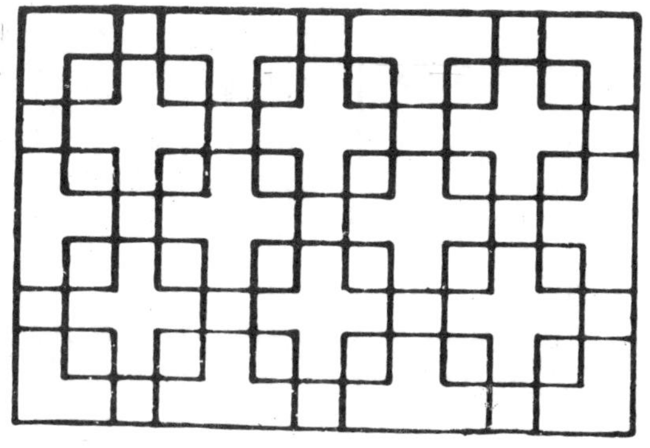

Fine and attractive design of solid Iron bars For all purpose

Strong design of Indian style useful for Factories and Garden fancing.

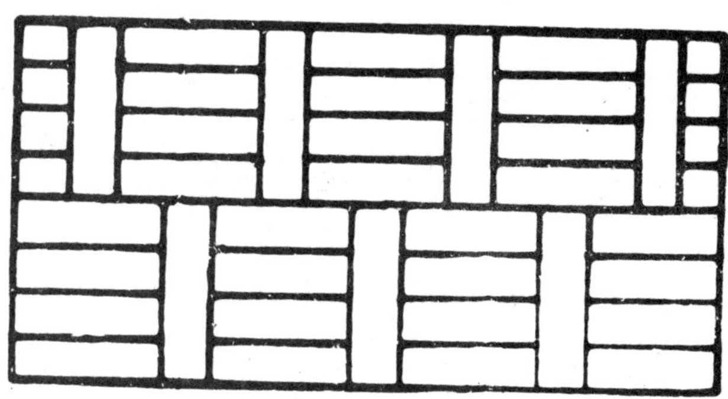

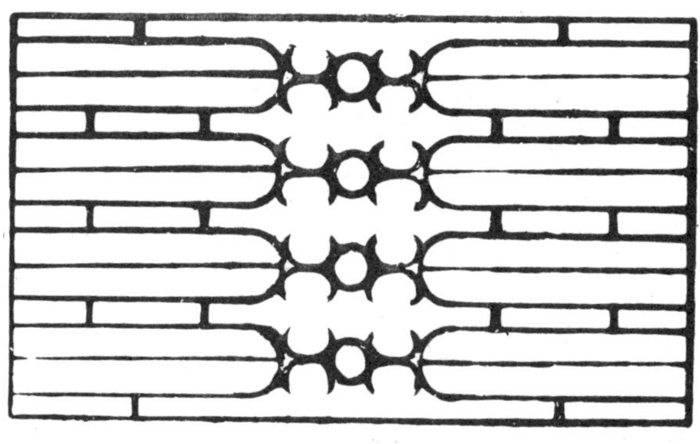

Modern Design based on Architectural construction.

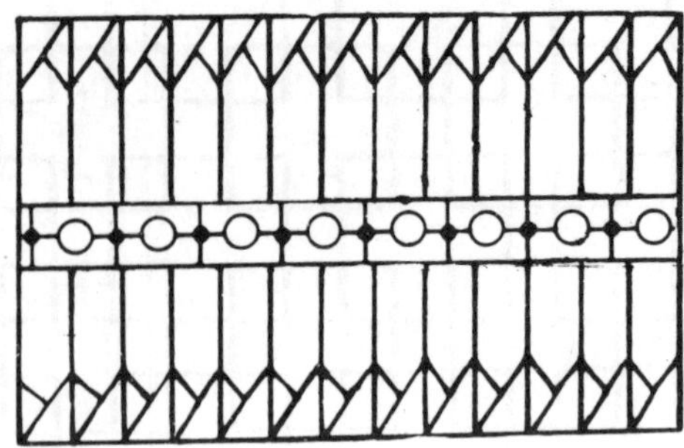

Modern and simple. type design using thinner flats and billas most suitable for latest types of building.

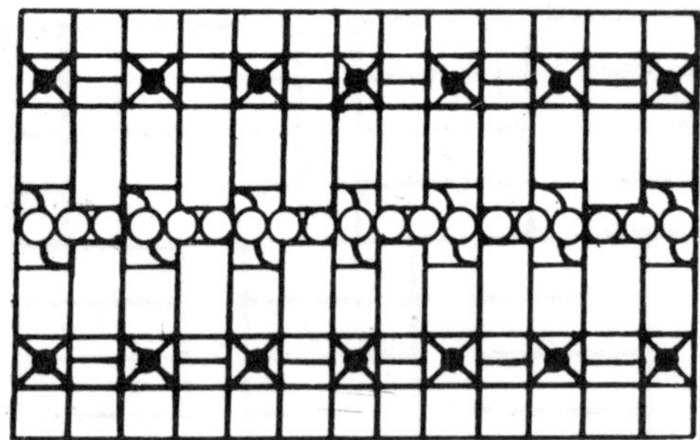

A composition of latest window Grill Design, the squares, "S" types and circles are used. The gap may be given according to the choice.

Best Tokeyo's design of Solid iron bars This is a close type design using "c" types and squares leaving the gap of 4" in the vertical position.

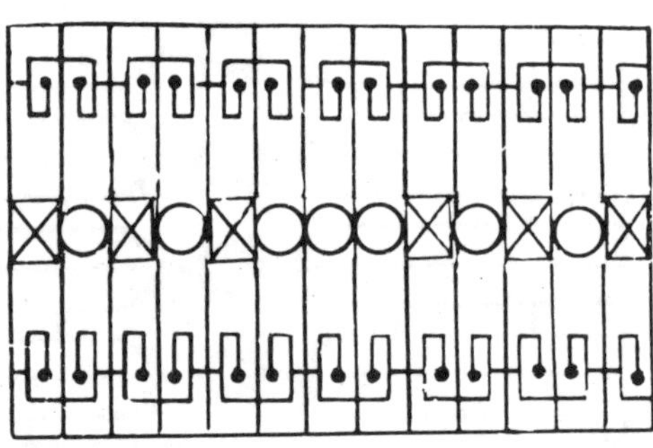

Universal design

Ornamental Designs on the Square Rods for the Decoration.

simple Design on the Square Rods for the Decoration.

beautiful design using diamonds, rectangular and other ornamentals.

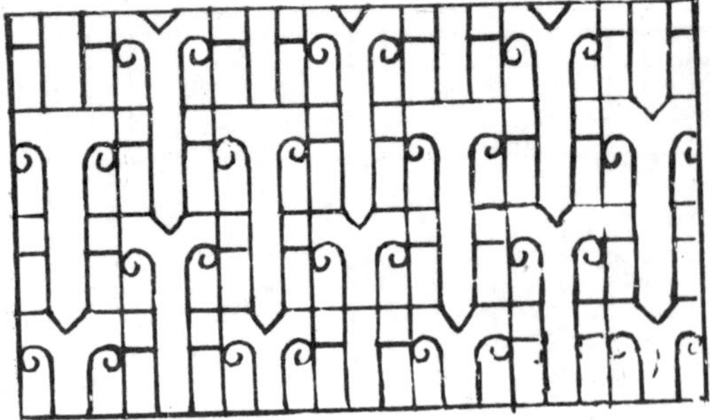

Design for Simple Beauty.
This type of design is suitable both for the domestic and industrial buildings.

Design for Modern Building.
In this window Grill Design, the squares, and circles are used.

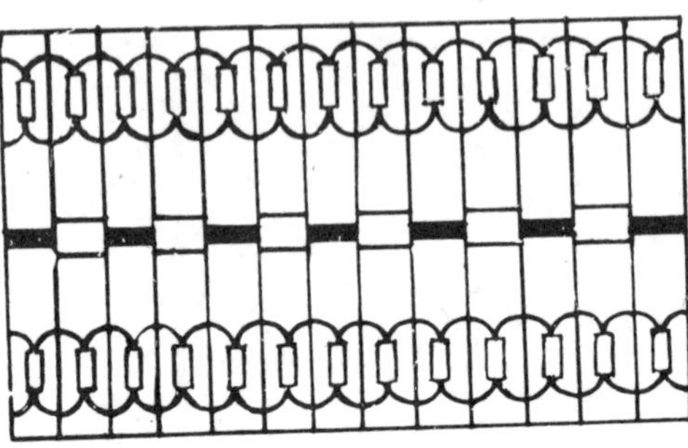

Switzerland Design for Window of Simple Beauty.
In this design, rectangulars, squares, and circles have been used.

Windows and Ventilators

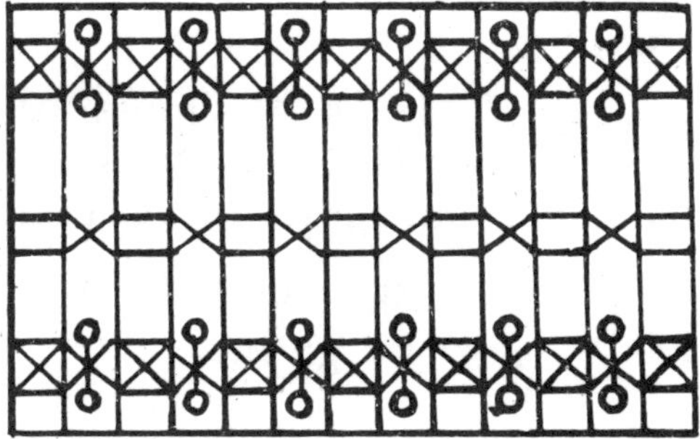

Beautiful Japanese Design. A common design using diamonds, rectangular and other ornamentals.

Very Beautiful simple and ornamental design. In the centre, simple and ornamental design has been used.

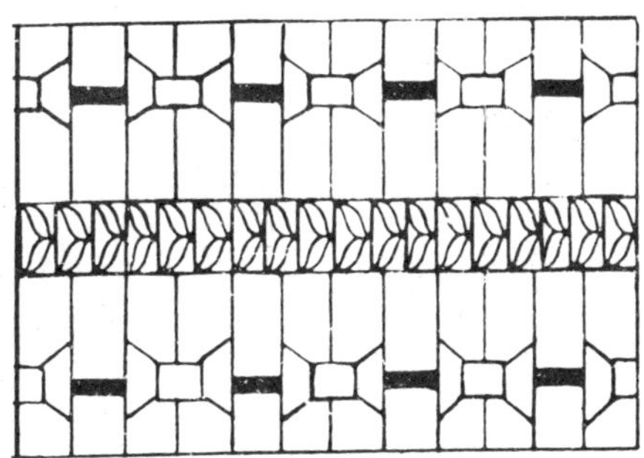

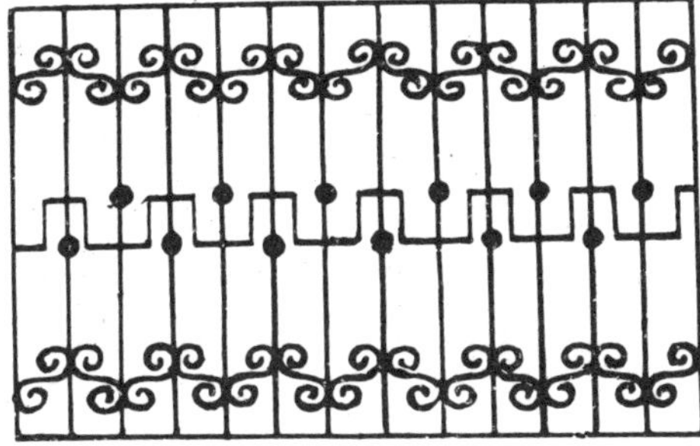

Best Japanies Design of solid Iron bars

In this design 'U and 'S' types have been used. The gap of 4" between two square rods or flates may be given for more strength

This is A simple basket type design of Window A gap of 4'' atleast between two square rods or flats may be given,

Good Beautiful and attractive design with a closer space in the bottom. Square rods or heavy section flats may be used.

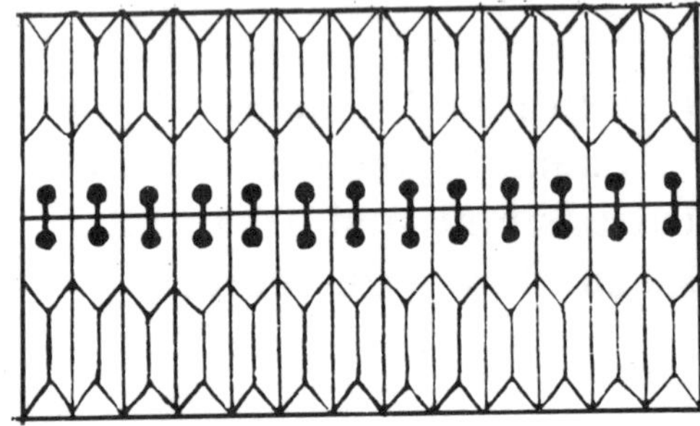

New Dacoration Peace of latest type design using diamonds, rectangular and other ornamentals.

Grill designs of old style.

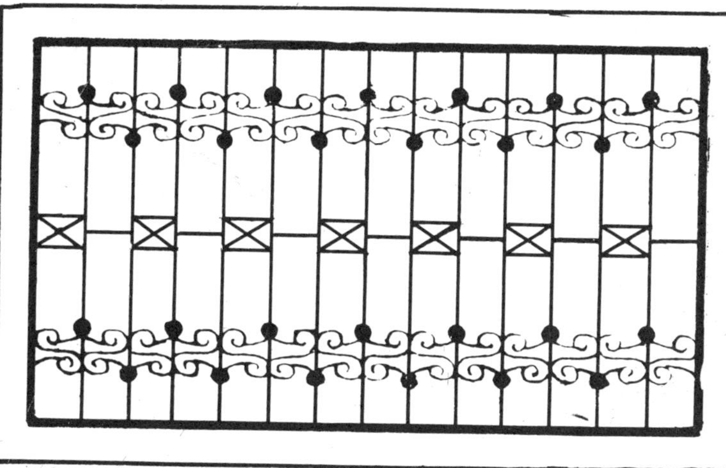

This is a simple and ornamental design. used In the Centre,

Art of Mughal Period Designs

Best and universal design of steel sheet cutting and solid iron bars.

Modern Designs of M. S. Wrought Iron Grill.

Beautiful Window

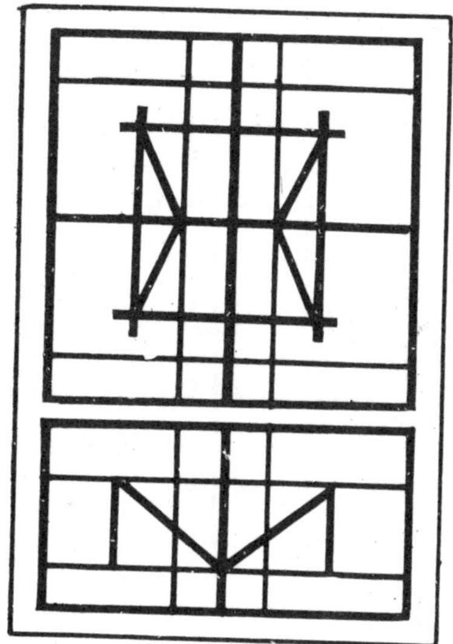

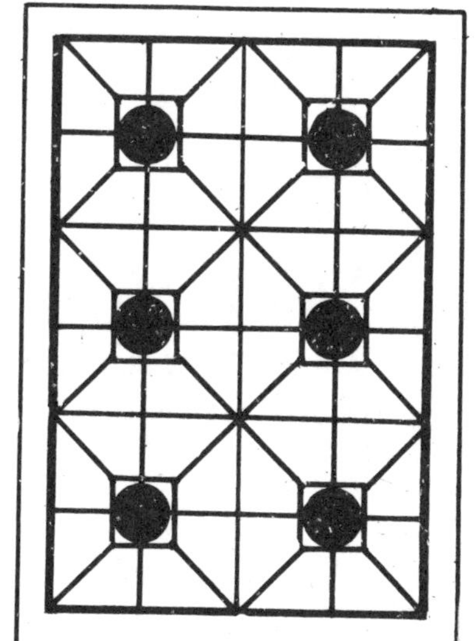

Italian design of Grills for Beautiful decoration.

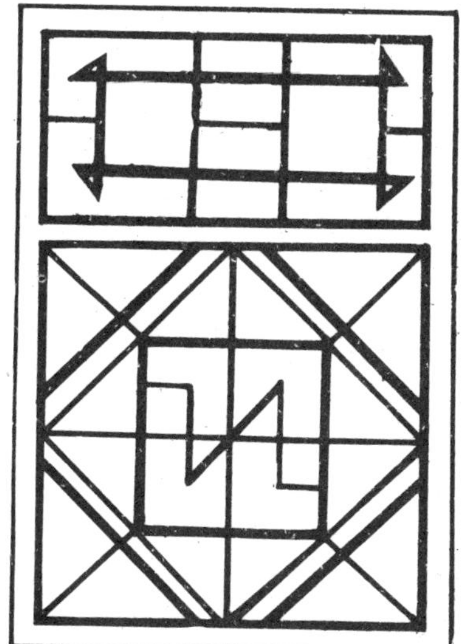

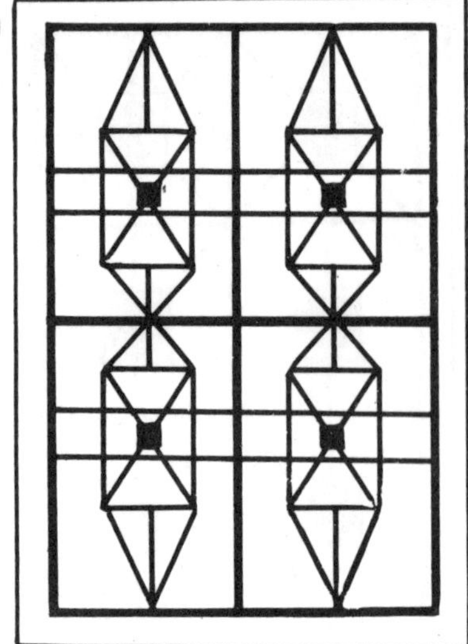

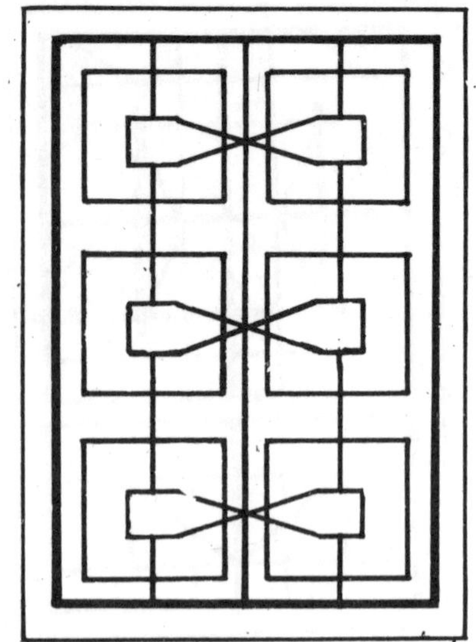

Designs of Long Iron bars British architectural for Big Embassy.

Style of Switzerland design for window,

Latest and Ultra-Modern Designs of England.

Attractive Moder Designs based on Folk Art.

Russian Grill design for Exhibition purpose.

Attractive and charming design of window

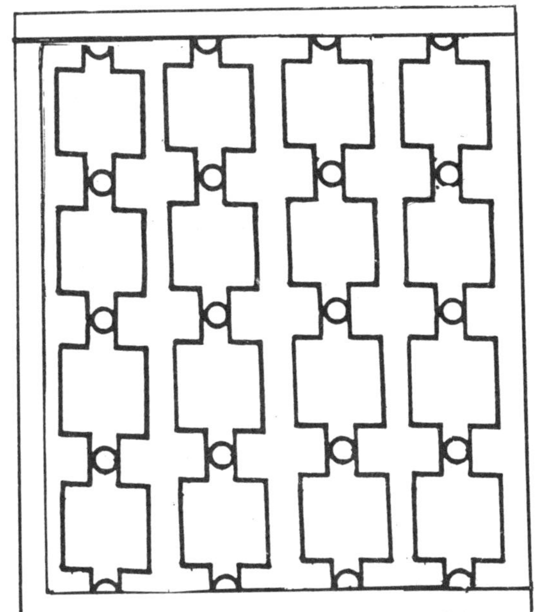

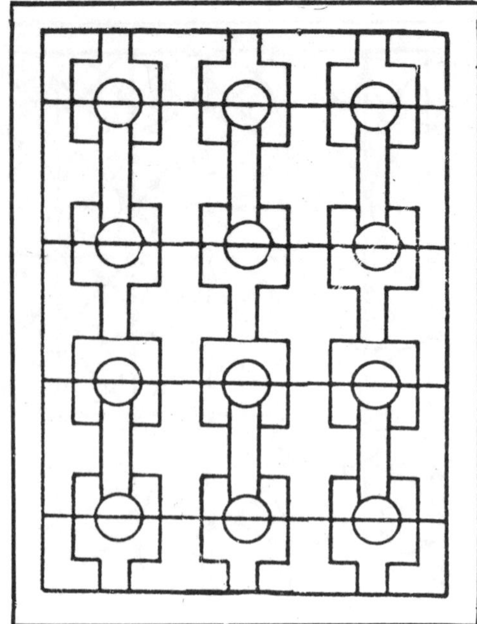

Leaves welded in between simple circles are the main characteristic of this design.

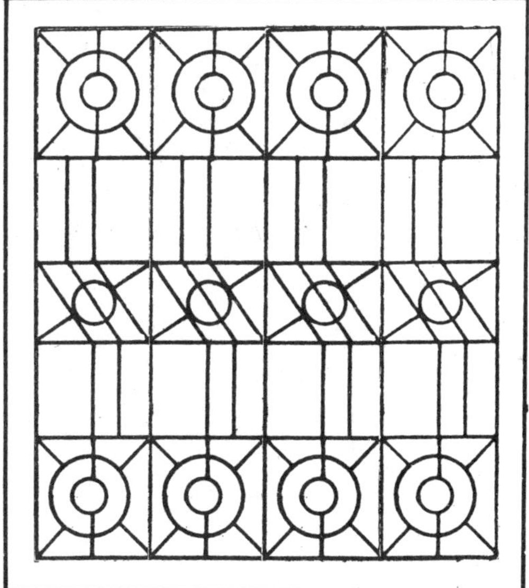
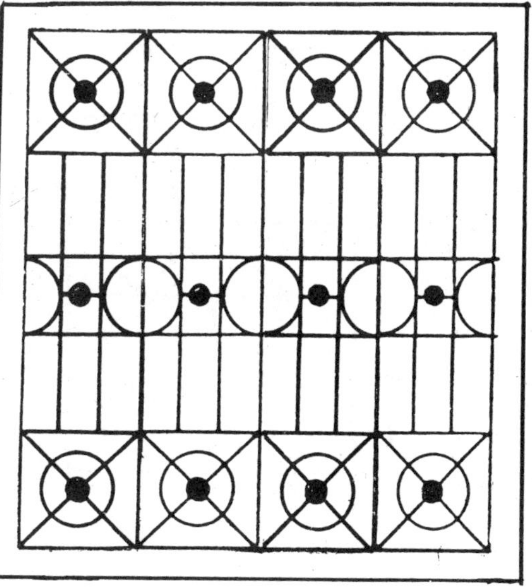

American design for Artistic designed Building.

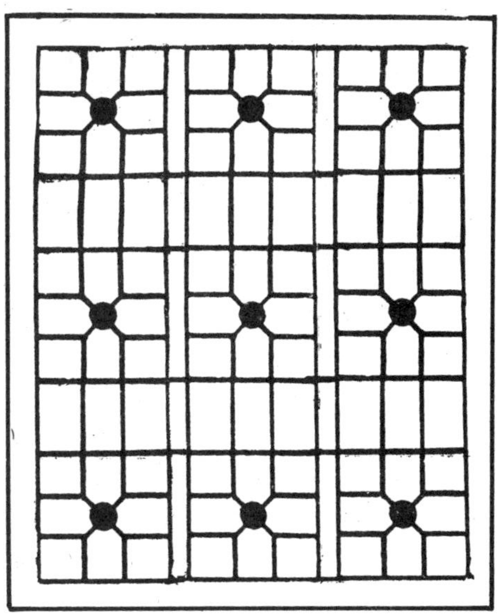

Beautiful Window

A composition of Best and latest design of modern style.

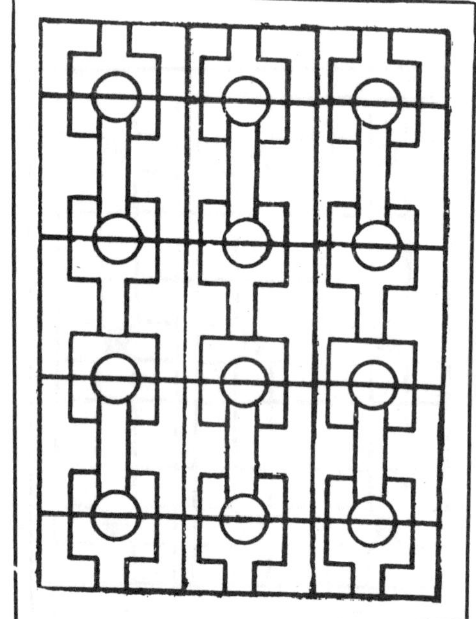

A composition of modern designs

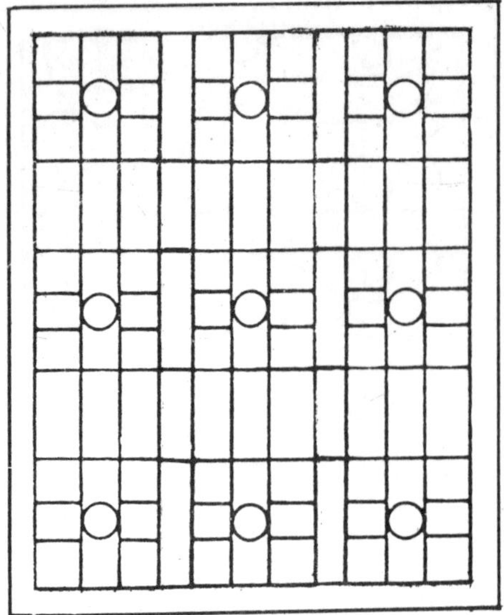

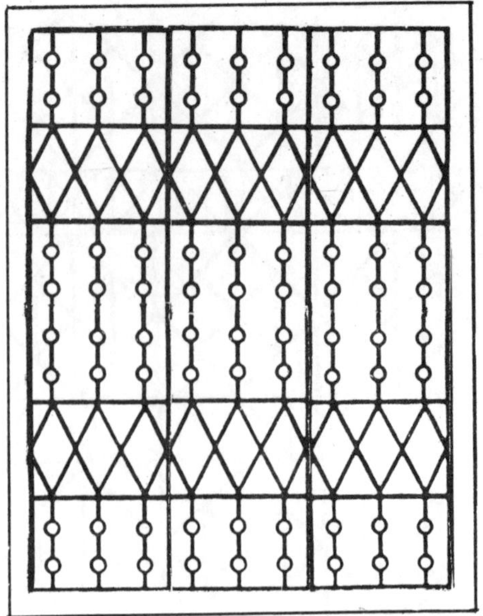

Latest designs of for window new Bunglow

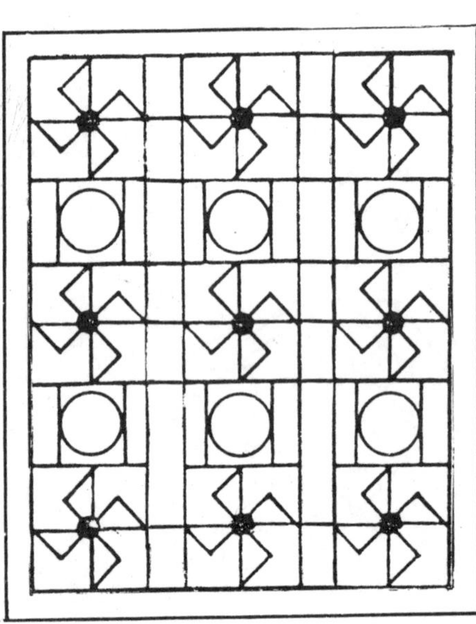

This complete design gives idea and art of the Mughal

Latest design of window Grills.

Beautiful Window Grilles,

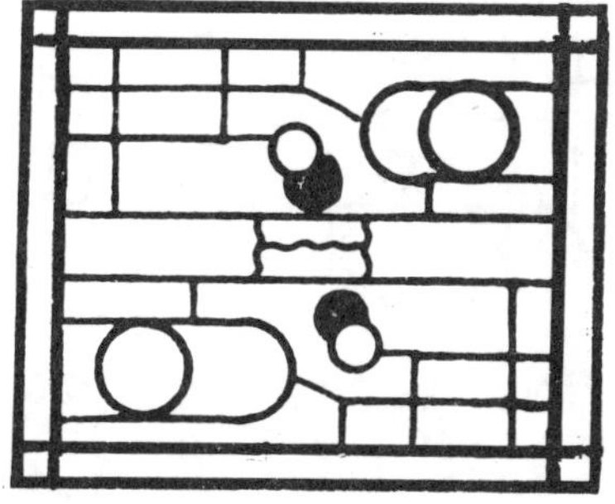

Common designs for commercial House Residential Building, Shop and Factories etc.

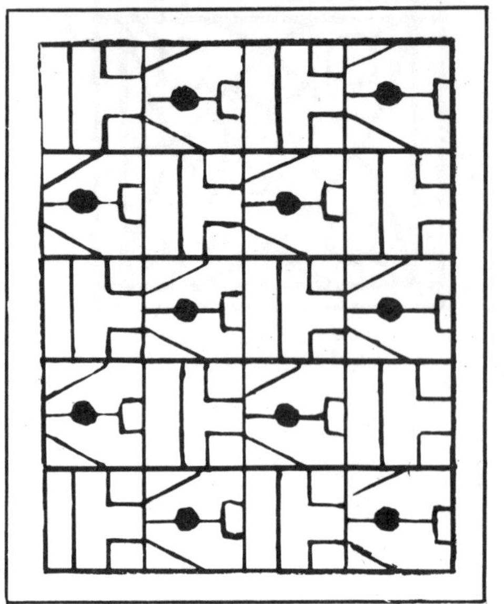

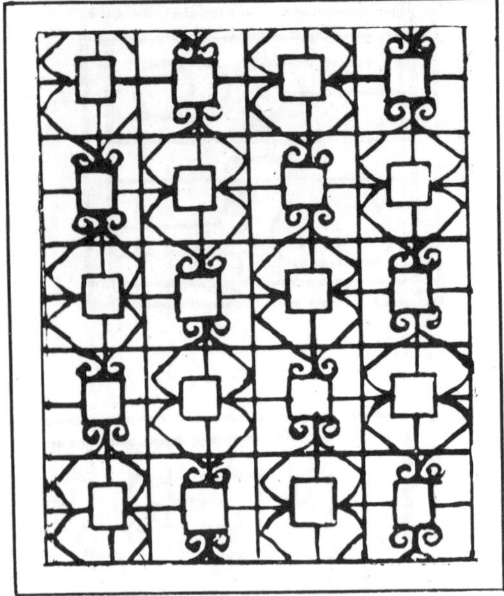

Australian design of Gate, Window and Railing Grills for Newly Constructed House.

WindowS

Switzerland design for window Grill.

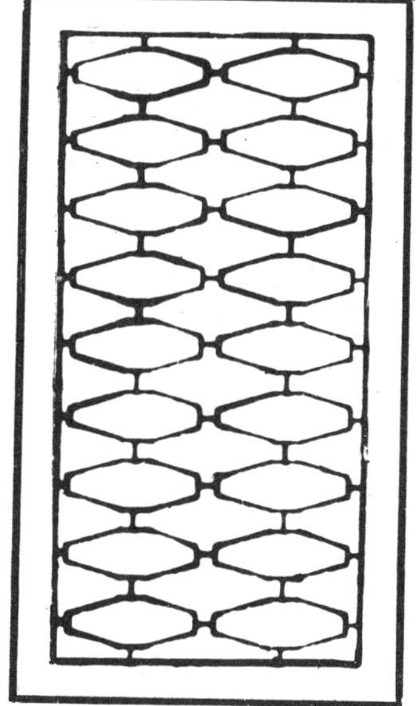

Universal window designs

Ancient designs for old style Buildings.

window Grill.

Japanese designs for new Bunglow.

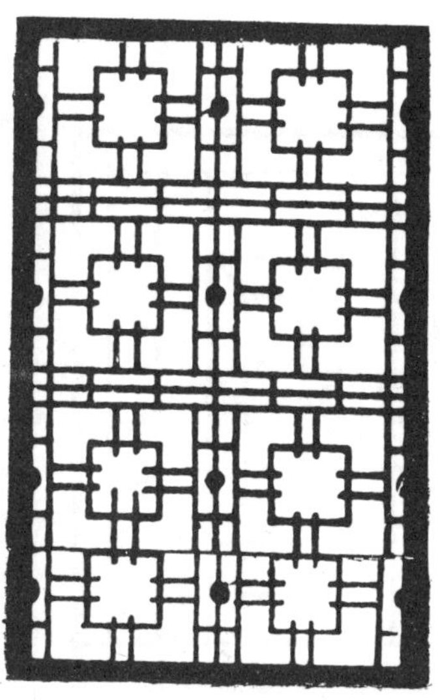

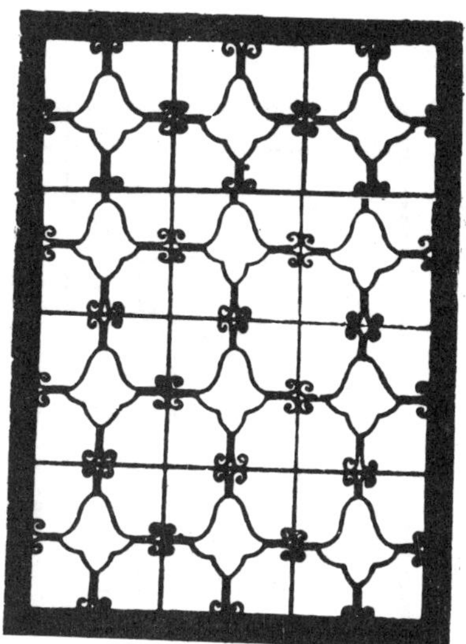

Beautiful Window

Ancientl Design of Grills increases the beauty of Small or Big Building.

Symitrical setting of Semicircle and straight Iron bars design. for window Grill

Windows and Ventilators

West Germany's Designs of Windows and Ventilators for New Decoration.

Beautiful Window

Leaves welded in betweens quare fraim of Iron are the main character of this design.

Ancient Russian Grill design quite suitable for Exhibition purpose etc.

Japanese designs for new Bunglow.

Best Tokeyo's design of Solid iron bars for new Bunglow.

Modern design of Layers welded in between square frame of Iron are the main character of this design.

Symitrical setting of Semicircle and straight Iron bars design. for window Grill

Attractive and Modern Ancient Russian Grill design quite suitable for Exhibition purpose etc.

New design of Paris

window design is suitable both for the domestic and industrial buildings.

simple and straight cutting lines design of heavy section flats or square rods may be used for both vertical and horizontal positions.

Japan's design for beauty

Rounded circle Designs, made of solid iron bars of window with net adjustment for Decoration.

Easy, simple and cheap Straight Iron bar designs with symitrical construction.

Two universal window Grill designs.

Latest German designs of M. S. wrought Iron bars with still and rod pieces insertion.

Modern design of Rods, welded in bet-weens quare fraim of Iron are the main character of this design.

Two pairs of modern designs

These designs shows the Idea of British Ancient Art suitable for office, College and School Buildings.

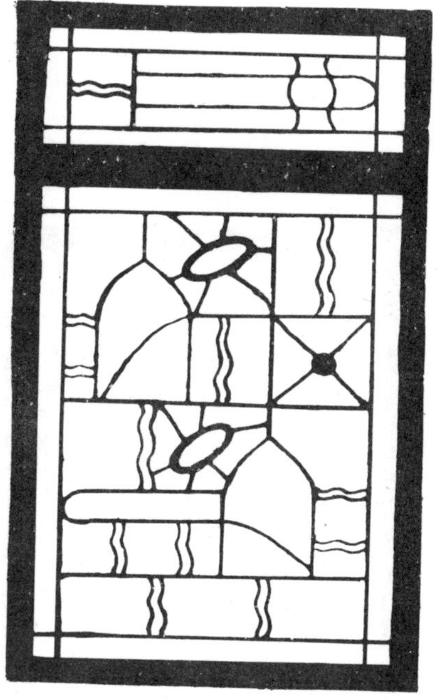

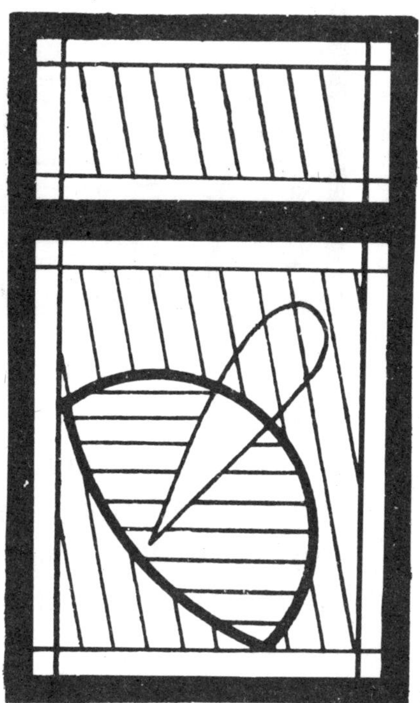

Latest design of door grills of Vertical Iron bars designs for well Planned Building.

Two pairs of modern designs

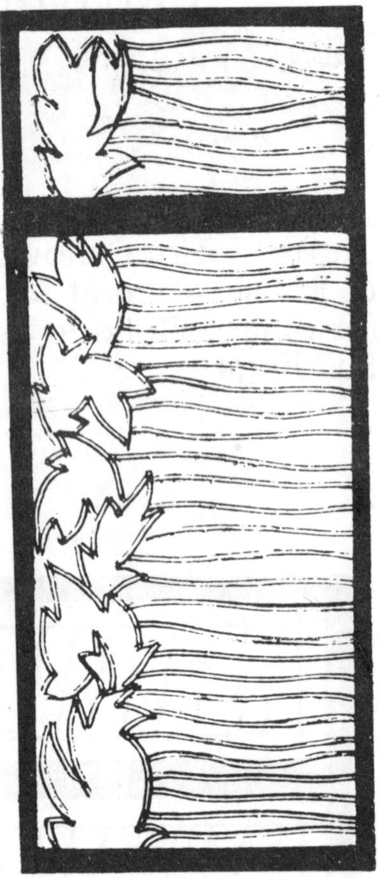

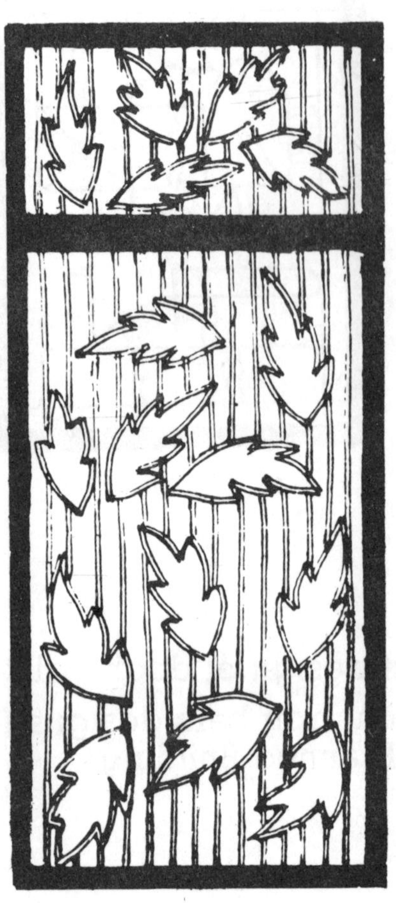

Modern design of Leaves welded in bet-weens quare fraim of Iron are the main character of this desian

Latest design of window Grills.

Round Iron bar designs in layer style, welded on the frames.

Tokeyo's design
of Solid iron bars

Latest and universal iron bars, design of famous Indian style for Strong Construction.

Architectural design of solid Square bar frame.

8 **Latest** simple type desgin The gap may be given according to the width of Window for more strength and support to this beautiful design.

This design suits for all the types of Buildings.

Modern style Design
gives an idea and
Art of Mughal Period.

Attractive and Modern
Ancient Russian Grill
design quite suitable
for Exhibition purpose

Switzerland design for window Grill.

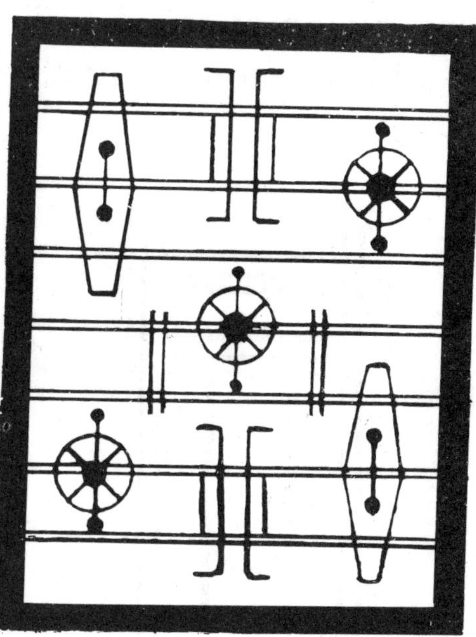

Attractive Iron Grill first designed in Germany.

Different design of iron bar in circle and harmonic curve.

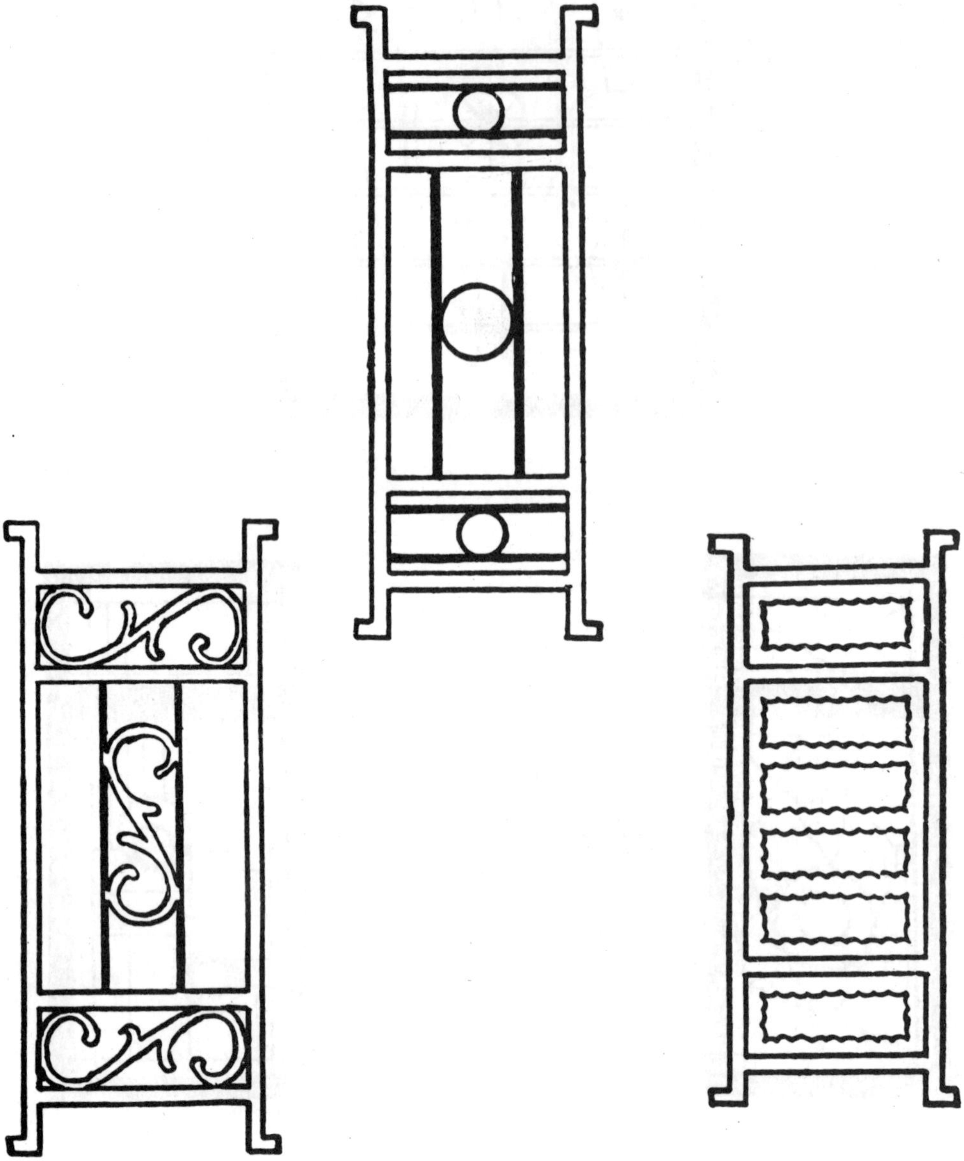

Window

Latest design of window for new construction.

Very good symitrycal setting of semi-circle Design.

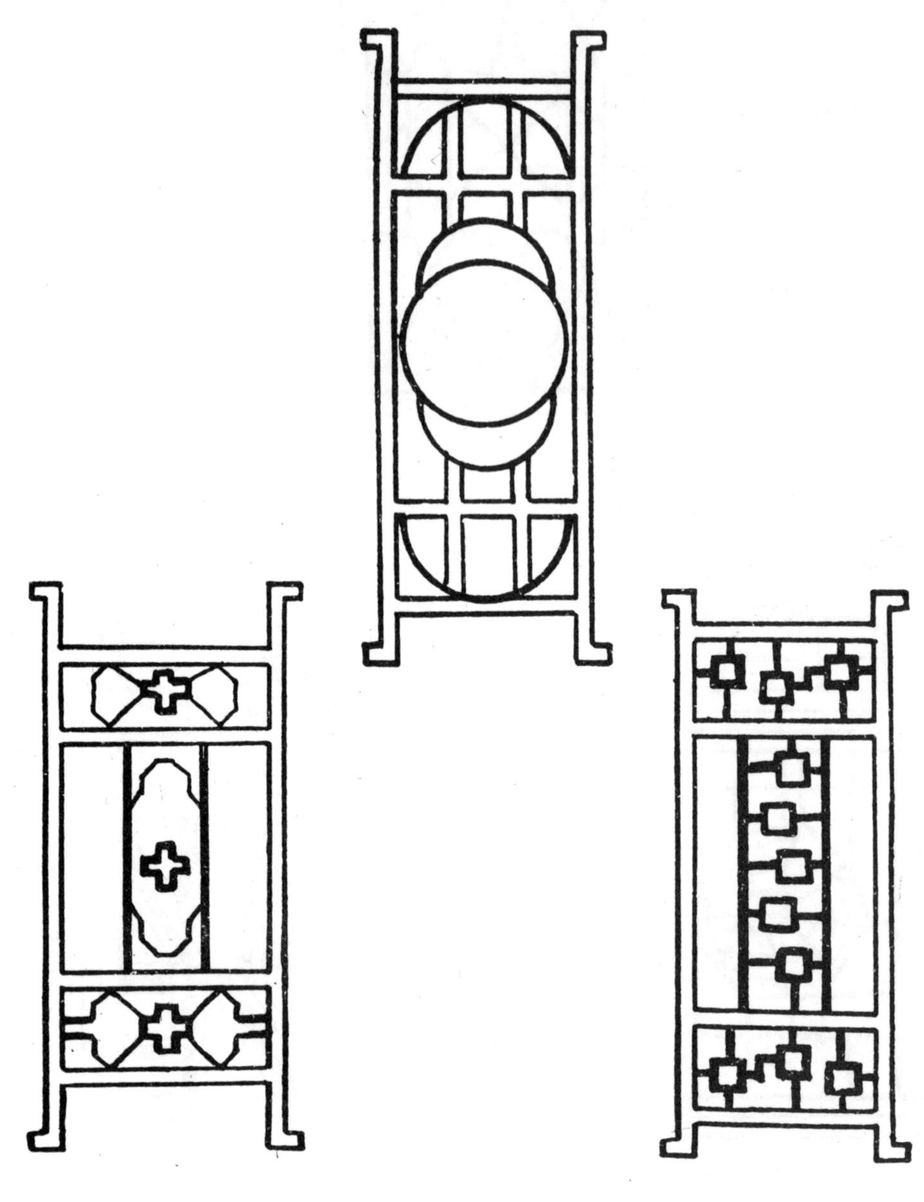

Simple latest design suits for all the latest types of buildings. The gap may be given according to the choice for safety, and more strength.

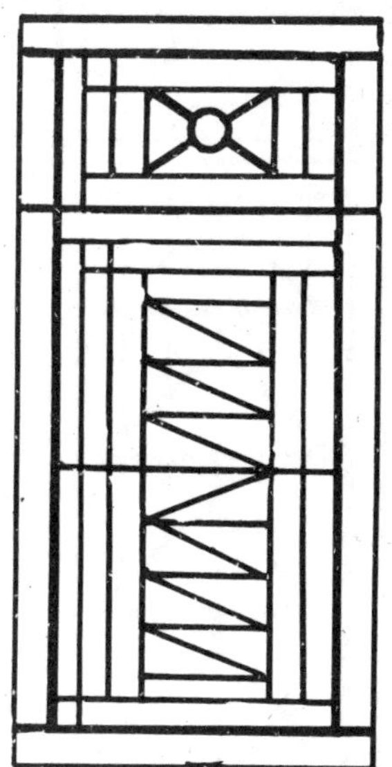

Architectural Grill Designs. Straight Iron bar

Design of triangles and squares with fully support for more strength

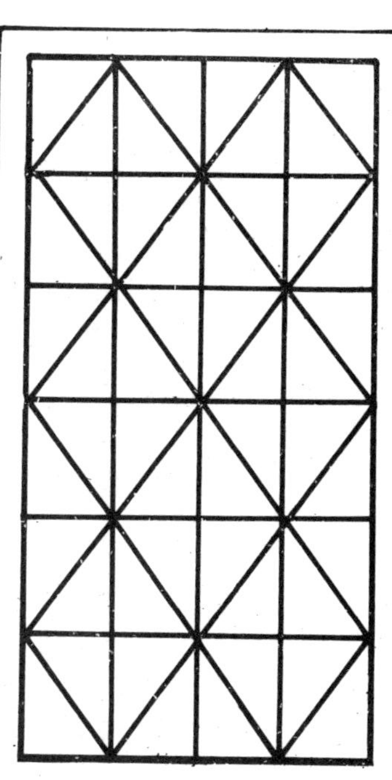

Architectural design

Architectural Grill design quite suitable for Exhibition purpose

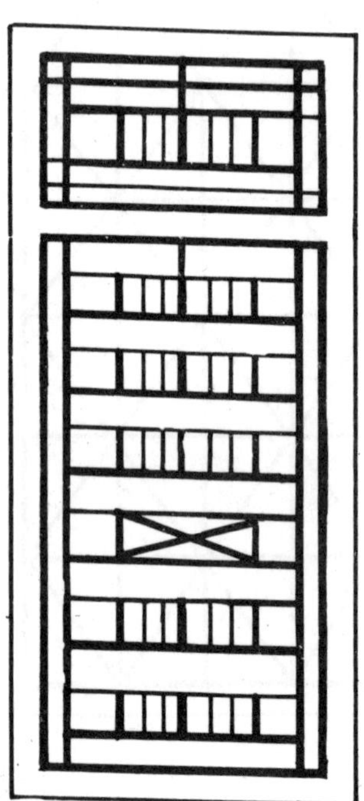

Modern designs of small pieces of solid iron bars

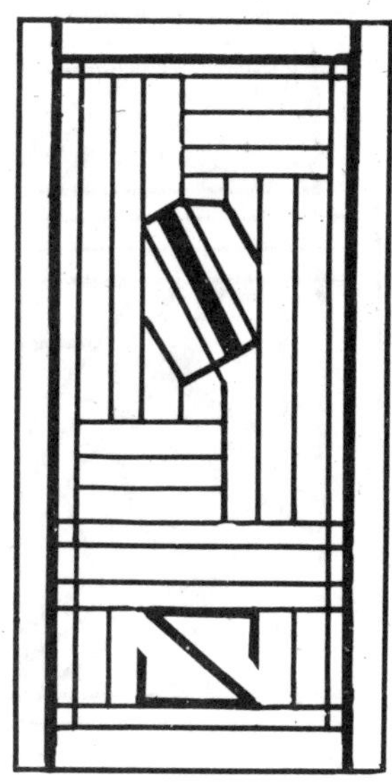

New Sample of Latest German designs Residential

A Common design for commercial House, Residential Building, Shop and Factories etc.

New Design of West Germany for biggest and Latest Construction.

New window Grill Design, the squares, iron bars and circles are used. The gap may be given according to the choice.

Leaving Gap of 4" between Two square Rods

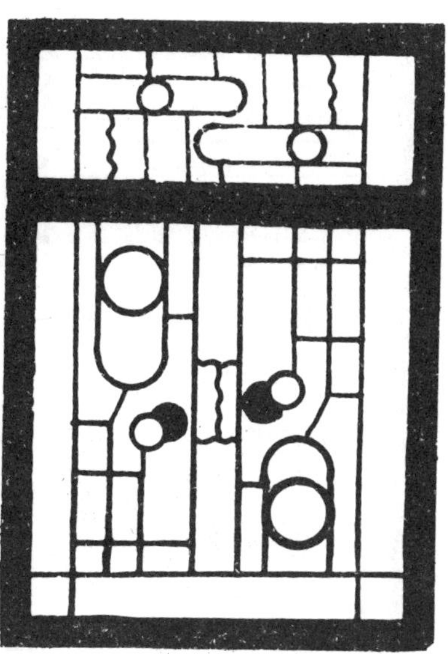

Beautiful Window

Modern design of window and railing.

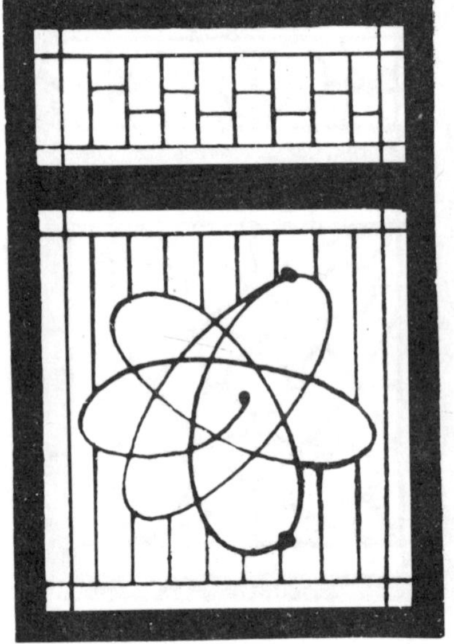

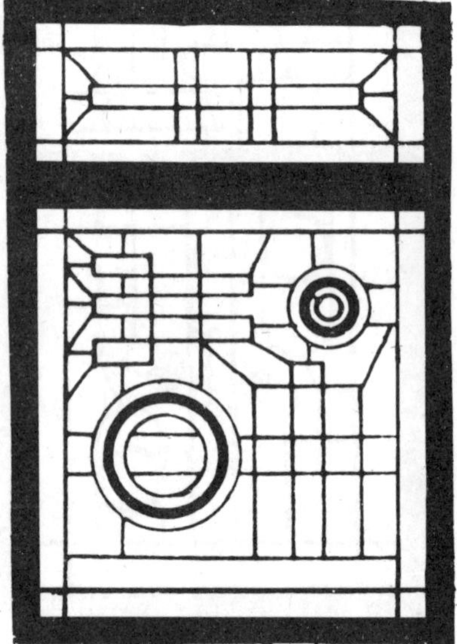

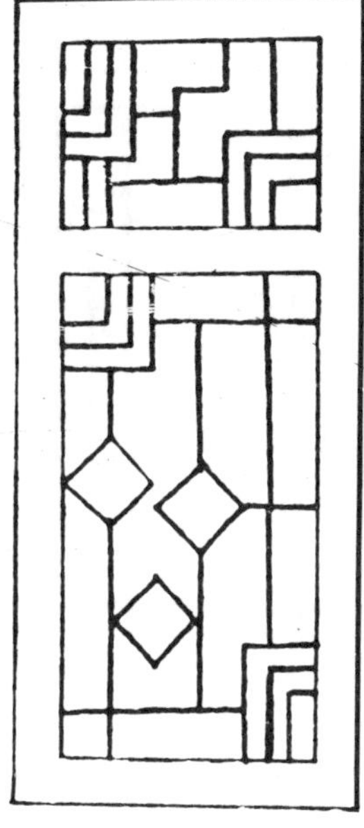

Old Design
for Strong
Construction.

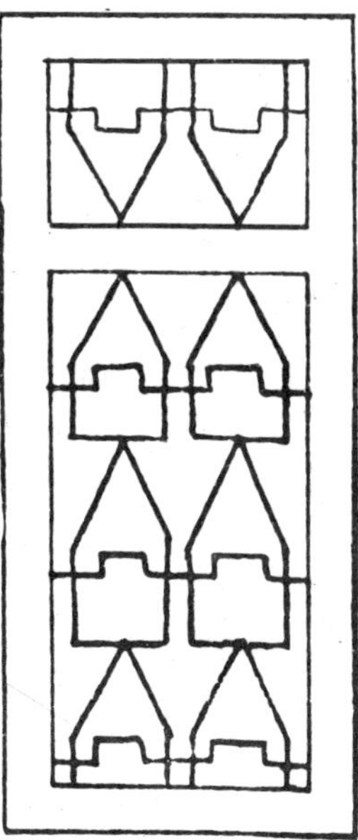

Best and universal design of steel sheet cutting and solid iron bars.

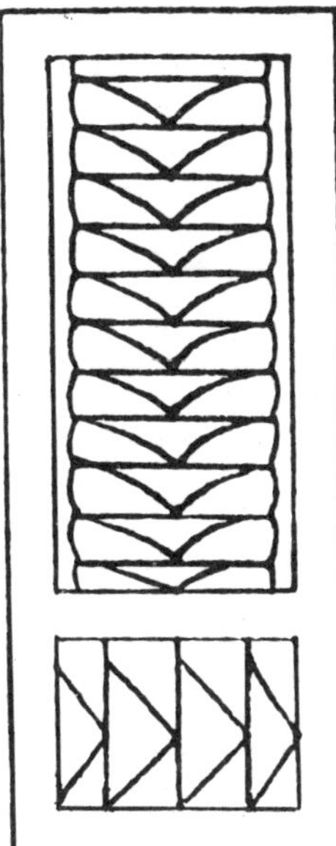

Attractive and charming design of window

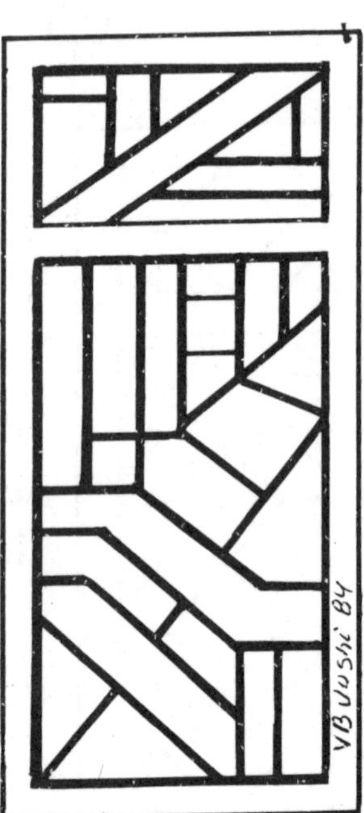

Ancient design of window for Decoration.

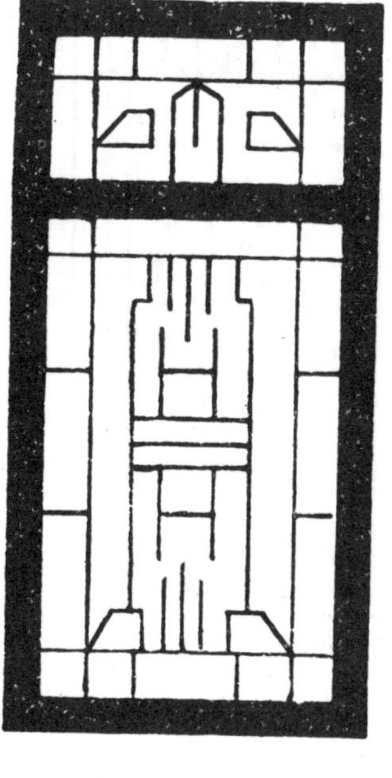

Thick and thin
vertical
Straight Iron
bar designs

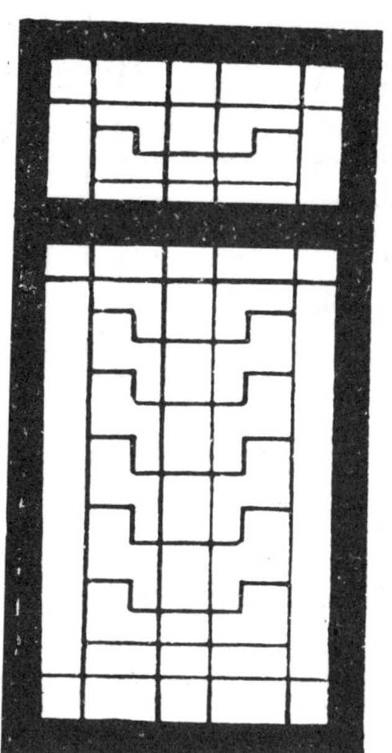

Latest
simple designs
with
symitrical

Very strong designs for decoration of residential and commercial building.

Universal design for Good Building

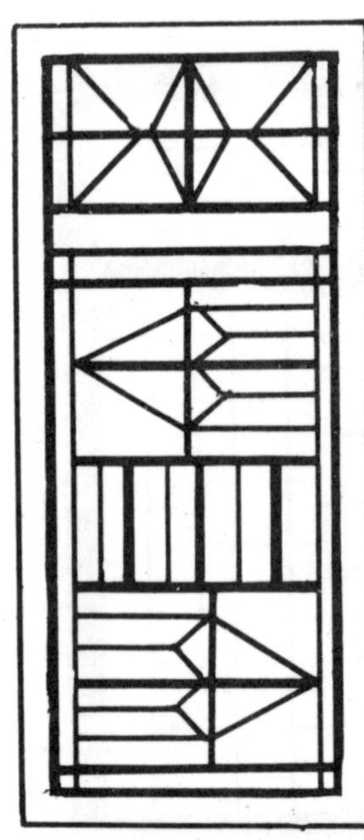

Windows and Ventilats

Latest design of window Grills.

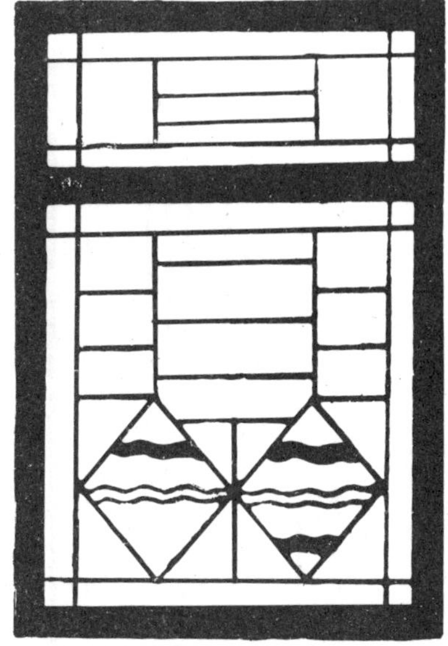

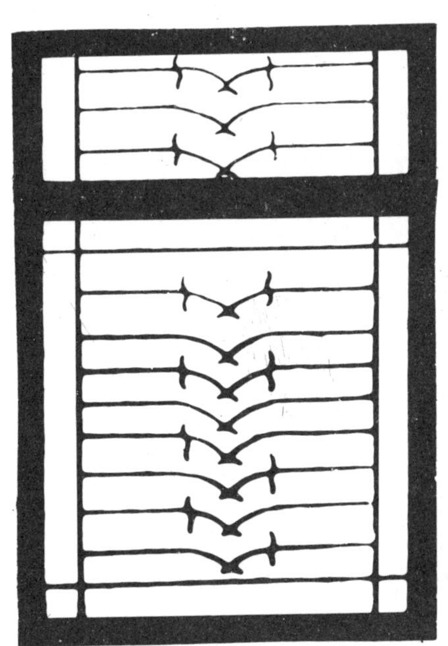

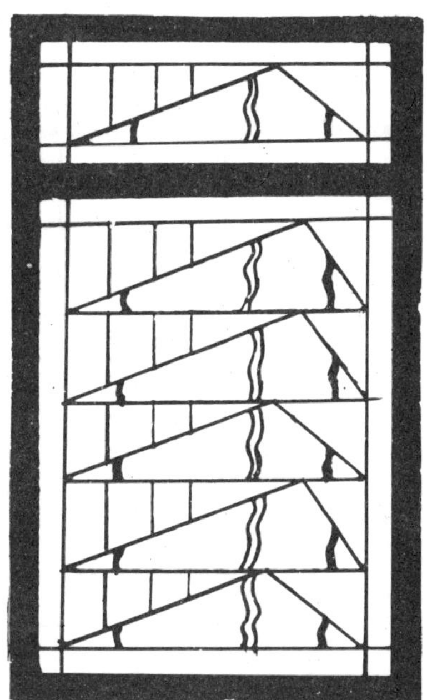

Modern designs gives an idea and art of the Mughal period.

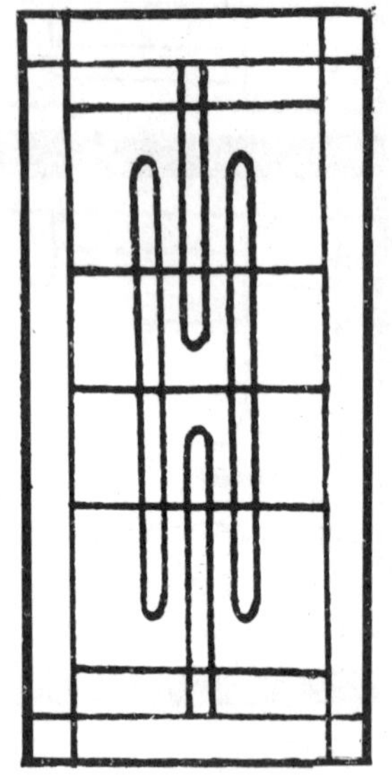

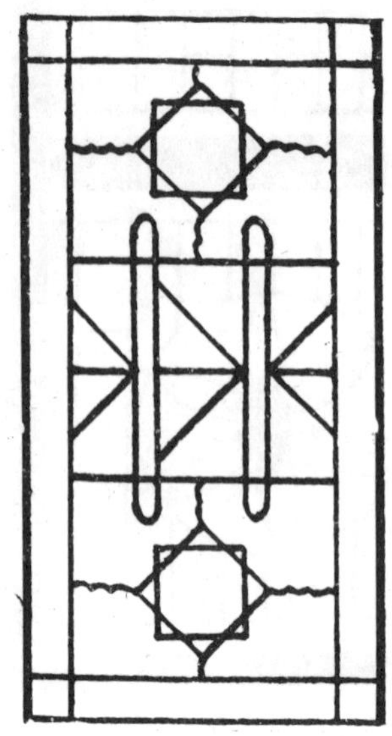

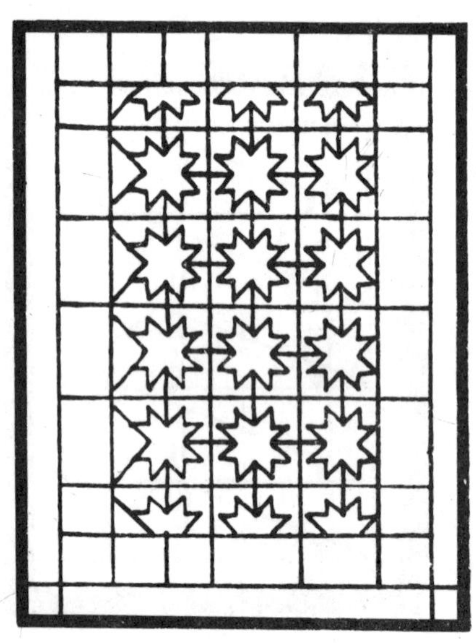